# English Grammar for Students of Latin

**The Study Guide
for Those Learning Latin**

*Second edition*

**Norma Goldman
Ladislas Szymanski**

The Olivia and Hill Press®

ENGLISH GRAMMAR series

*English Grammar for Students of French*
*English Grammar for Students of Spanish*
*English Grammar for Students of German*
*English Grammar for Students of Italian*
*English Grammar for Students of Russian*
*English Grammar for Students of Japanese*
*Gramática española para estudiantes de inglés*

© 1993, Jacqueline Morton

Printed in the U.S.A.

Library of Congress Catalog Card Number: 82-80514

ISBN 0-934034-19-2

# CONTENTS

# To the Student

**English Grammar for Students of Latin** explains the grammatical terms that are in your Latin textbook and shows you how they relate to English grammar. Once you have understood the terms and concepts in your own language, it will be easier for you to undertand your textbook. With simple explanations and numerous examples this handbook compares English and Latin grammar, pointing out the similarities and differences.

Most teachers incorporate **English Grammar** into the class syllabus so you will know which pages to read before doing an assignment in your Latin textbook. If you are selecting the pages yourself, check the detailed index for the terms and concepts you will need to understand for your assignment. When you finish a chapter in the handbook, you can test your comprehension by doing the short Reviews and checking your answers against the Answer Key.

### Tips for Studying a Foreign Language

1. RULES — Make sure you understand each rule before you move on to the next one. Language learning is like building a house; each brick is only as secure as its foundation.

2. MEMORIZATION — All languages require memory work. There are many ways you can memorize.

- Make vocabulary cards or lists of words for each chapter. If you make cards, use color coding, keeping different parts of speech on different color cards.

- Put Latin on one side, with principal parts for verbs and the nomi-native, genitive, and gender for nouns. Put the English meanings on the reverse side. A friend can help you drill, but it is easy to drill yourself.

- Use different colored inks for masculine, feminine, or neuter nouns.

- When you memorize vocabulary meanings, remember that an English derivative can be helpful, but is not always the best translation.

- Shuffle the cards before reviewing, and remove the cards as you master them so that you can concentrate on unlearned words.

- Memorize rules aloud: e.g. "The relative pronoun takes its gender and number from its antecedent, but takes its case from its use in its own clause," and think about what the rule means as you say it.

For some students, listing vocabulary words on a piece of paper or in a notebook, dividing them by parts of speech, can be as helpful as making and drilling with vocabulary cards, but most students seem to prefer the cards. One can buy sets of printed Latin vocabulary cards, but students need specific words geared to the vocabulary in the text. The more words you know, the easier it will be to read a passage. This grammar book will help you understand how the words are used in English and Latin sentences.

## ACKNOWLEDGEMENTS

The authors wish to acknowledge their gratitude to the Word Processing Center at Wayne State University under the able direction of David Nelson for its practical and professional help. We thank the Office of Research and Sponsored Programs for the grants that have provided the funds for typing the Revised Edition. We are indebted to Thomas Moeller and to Anthony Di Ponio for their computing skills in solving disk problems. We also thank Anika Terrell, our Student Assistant, for her typing skills, her knowledge of Latin, and careful eye in preparation of the text. We wish to thank Jacqueline Morton, and her capable assistant, Stéphanie DiTullio, for their patience and helpful advice in the preparation of this manuscript. Most of all, however, we thank Dr. Edith M. A. Kovach for her critical reading of the Revised Edition, her discriminating judgement, her precise use of language, and the many helpful suggestions she has provided.

Norma Goldman

Ladislas Szymanski

## INTRODUCTION

Learning a foreign language, in this case, Latin, requires that you look at each word in three ways:

1. The **meaning** of the word—An English word must be connected with a Latin word which has equivalent meaning.

*Girl* has basically the same meaning as the Latin word **puella.**

Words with equivalent meanings are learned by memorizing vocabulary. Because so many English words come from Latin, it is often your knowledge of English that will help you memorize Latin words.

| Latin | Meaning | English derivative |
|-------|---------|--------------------|
| fīlius | son | filial |
| īnsula | island | insulate |
| fāma | fame | fame |

*Son* has the same meaning as the Latin word **fīlius. Fīlius** and *filial* are called **cognates,** that is, words in different languages which are related to each other because they are based on a common stem or root (**fili-**). The English word *filial,* as in "filial love" (the love of a child for a parent), will help you associate it with the Latin word **fīlius.**

Occasionally knowing one Latin word will help you learn another.

Knowing that **fīlius** is *son* will help you learn that **fīlia** is *daughter.*

Sometimes there is little similarity between Latin words of related meaning, and knowing one will not help you learn another. Therefore, you will have to learn each vocabulary item separately.

Knowing that **fēmina** is *woman* will not help you learn that **vir** is *man.*

In addition there are times when words in combination take on a special meaning. These expressions, called idioms, are unique to a language. It is not the meaning of the individual word, or words, which is important, but the overall meaning. For instance, to say "thank you" Latin uses an equivalent expression.

**Tibi grātiās habeō.**
Literally: "I have thanks to you."

2. The **class** of the word—Words are grouped by types, each type being called a **part of speech**. Here is a list of the eight different parts of speech:

| | |
|---|---|
| noun | verb |
| pronoun | adverb |
| adjective | preposition |
| conjunction | interjection |

Each part of speech has its own rules for use. You must learn to identify the part of speech of each word so that you will know what rules to apply.

Look at the word *love* in the following sentences:

The students *love* to learn the language.
    verb

My *love* is like a red, red rose.
  noun

He is famous for writing *love* stories.
       adjective

The English word is the same in all three sentences, but in Latin three different words, each following a different set of rules, must be used because each *love* belongs to a different part of speech.

3. The **use** of the word—A word must be identified according to the role it plays in the sentence. Each word, whether English or Latin, serves a unique function within the sentence. Determining this use or **function** will help you to find the proper Latin equivalent. Look at the word *her* in the following sentences:

All the students admire *her*.
      direct object

The teacher gave *her* an "A."
     indirect object

Are you going to graduate with *her?*
      object of preposition *with*

*Her* work is excellent.
 adjective

In English the word is the same in all four sentences, but in Latin four different words, each following a different set of rules, must be used because the word *her* has four different uses.

## *Nota Bene (Note well, abbreviated N.B.)*

As a student of Latin you must learn to recognize both the part of speech and the function of a word within a sentence. This is essential because words in Latin have great influence on each other.

*The beautiful small **islands** are in the large Mediterranean Sea.*

Parvae īnsulae pulchrae sunt in magnō marī Mediterrāneō.

### IN ENGLISH

The only word that affects another is **islands**, which affects *are*. If the word were *island*, the verb *are* would be *is*.

### IN LATIN

The word for *islands* (**īnsulae**) affects not only *are* (**sunt**), but also the words for *beautiful* (**pulchrae**) and *small* (**parvae**). The word for *sea* (**marī**) affects the equivalent words for *large* (**magnō**) and *Mediterranean* (**Mediterrāneō**). The only word unaffected by the other words is the prepostion *in* (**in**), but it affects the word *sea* (**marī**).

Since parts of speech and their use are usually determined in the same way in English and Latin, as well as all the Romance languages (French, Spanish, Portuguese, Italian, and Romanian), this handbook will show you how to identify them in English. You will then learn to compare English and Latin constructions. This will give you a better understanding of the explanations in your Latin textbook.

# 1. WHAT IS A NOUN?

A **noun** is a word that can be the name of:

- a person      girl, teacher, god, Minerva, Jupiter
- an animal     bull, Cerberus
- a place       island, city, state, country, Rome, Italy
- a thing       map, sea, picture, star, island
- an event      graduation, marriage, birth, death, robbery
- an idea       peace, war, democracy, love, virtue, luxury
  or concept

As you can see, a noun is not only a word which names something that is tangible, i.e., that you can touch, such as *map* and *bull,* it can also be the name of things that are abstract, i.e, that you cannot touch, such as *peace* and *love.*

**IN ENGLISH**
Nouns that always begin with a capital letter, such as the names of people and places are called **proper nouns**. Nouns that do not begin with a capital letter *(peace, love, professor, dog)* are called **common nouns**.

> The *king* of *gods* and *men* was *Jupiter.*
>    common common   common   proper
>    noun    noun     noun     noun

A noun that is made up of two words is called a **compound noun**. A compound noun can be a common noun, such as *ice cream*, or a proper noun such as *North Africa*. To help you recognize nouns, here is a paragraph where the nouns are in *italics.*

> The *Romans,* at the *time* of the *Empire,* imported *goods* from *countries* around the *Mediterranean Sea.* Fancy inlaid *furniture* manufactured in *Asia Minor* decorated the *rooms* of the wealthy *Romans,* while Greek *statues* and finely painted *vases* decorated the *garden* and *atrium. Spices* for *foods* and *medicines* made up a great *market* in *Rome,* and *marble* in various *colors* was imported to decorate the *temples.* The unfavorable *balance* of *trade* was so serious a *problem* under the *Emperor Vespasian* that he set up a special *investigation* to find out why *Rome* was sending out so much *money* for *imports.*

**IN LATIN**
Nouns generally have the same function that they have in English.

▼▼▼▼▼▼▼▼▼▼▼▼▼▼REVIEW ▼▼▼▼▼▼▼▼▼▼▼▼▼▼▼▼

Circle the nouns in the following sentences.

1. Diana was the goddess of the moon.
2. Phoebus Apollo, her twin brother, was the god of the sun.
3. Mars was the god of war.
4. Juno was goddess of marriage and childbirth.
5. These deities lived on Mt. Olympus, and thus they were called the Olympians.

## 2. WHAT IS MEANT BY GENDER?

**Gender** is the grammatical classification of a word as masculine, feminine, or neuter.

Here is a list of parts of speech that have gender:

| English | Latin |
|---|---|
| nouns | nouns |
| pronouns | pronouns |
| possessive adjectives | adjectives |

**IN ENGLISH**

While English nouns are not classified according to grammatical gender, some nouns have a **natural gender** based on the biological sex of the person or animal for which the noun stands. For instance, when we replace a proper or common noun with *he* or *she*, we automatically use *he* for males and *she* for females. Most nouns which name things that do not have a sex are replaced by *it*.

Nouns referring to males indicate the **masculine** gender.

> *Paul* came home; *he* was tired, and I was glad to see *him*.
>   noun        masculine               masculine
>   male

Nouns referring to females indicate the **feminine** gender.

> The *girl* came home; *she* was tired, and I was glad to see *her*.
>   noun      feminine               feminine
>   female

All other nouns which do not indicate a biological gender are considered **neuter.**

> The *city* of Washington is lovely. I enjoyed visiting *it*.
>   noun                       neuter

**IN LATIN**

Most nouns, common and proper, are masculine, feminine, or neuter. The gender of Latin nouns is either a natural gender, based on biological sex, or a grammatical gender, an artificial distinction where no sex is involved.

1. The gender of nouns based on **natural gender** is easy to determine. These are nouns whose meaning is always tied to one or the other of the biological sexes, male or female.

- all words referring to males are masculine

| | |
|---|---|
| deus | *god* |
| Iuppiter | *Jupiter* |
| puer | *boy* |

- all words referring to females are feminine

| | |
|---|---|
| māter | *mother* |
| fīlia | *daughter* |
| rēgīna | *queen* |

2. The gender of all other nouns, common and proper, cannot be explained in terms of sex. These nouns have only a **grammatical gender** which is unrelated to biological sex.

Many nouns that are neuter in English (objects, countries, rivers, cities, etc.) are either masculine or feminine gender in Latin, although some are neuter.[1]

Here are some examples of English nouns classified under the gender of their Latin equivalent.

| Masculine | Feminine | Neuter |
|---|---|---|
| book | boat | river |
| chariot | tree | temple |
| army | courage | gift |
| field | country | animal |
| mountain | Athens | example |
| foot | Rome | horn |

It is also helpful to know that names of rivers, winds, months, and mountains are masculine. Names of cities, countries, plants, trees, and most abstract qualities are feminine.

Gender can sometimes be determined by looking at the ending of the first form of a Latin noun as given in your vocabulary. Below are some noun endings which often correspond to the masculine, feminine, or neuter genders. Since you will see these endings frequently, it is worth being familiar with them, although exceptions do occur.

---

[1] In English we refer to a ship as "she" in a sentence like: "The Queen Elizabeth is in dock. *She* is a fine ship." We can thus understand the phenomenon of grammatical gender.

**Masculine endings**
-us    taurus *(bull)*, amīcus *(friend)*, Nīlus *(Nile)*, animus *(soul)*
-er    puer *(boy)*, ager *(field)*, Iuppiter *(Jupiter)*, pater *(father)*
-or    auctor *(author)*, ōrātor *(orator)*, victor *(victor)*, amor *(love)*

**Feminine endings**
-a    puella *(girl)*, fēmina *(woman)*, porta *(gate)*, glōria *(glory)*
-ās    vānitās *(vanity)*, aetās *(age)*, veritās *(truth)*
-dō    magnitūdo *(great size)*, fortitūdō *(strength)*, servitūdō *(slavery)*
-iō    regiō *(region)*, actiō *(action)*, religiō *(religion)*, notiō *(notion)*

**Neuter endings**
-um    templum *(temple)*, pōmum *(apple)*, dōnum *(gift)*
-men    flūmen *(river)*, agmen *(line of battle)*, nōmen *(name)*
-e    mare *(sea)*
-al    animal *(animal)*
-ar    exemplar *(example)*

## Nota Bene
It is important that you learn the gender of every Latin noun which
is introduced. A noun's gender is important not only for the noun
itself, but also for the gender of words which the noun influences:
pronouns, adjectives and participles.

▼▼▼▼▼▼▼▼▼▼▼▼▼▼▼REVIEW ▼▼▼▼▼▼▼▼▼▼▼▼▼▼▼▼▼

Using the endings listed above, classify the vocabulary entry of the
Latin nouns below by circling the gender masculine (M), feminine (F), or
neuter (N).

1. alumna *(graduate)*       M    F    N

2. alumnus *(graduate)*      M    F    N

3. templum *(temple)*        M    F    N

4. ōrātor *(orator)*          M    F    N

5. Dīana *(Diana)*            M    F    N

6. rosa *(rose)*              M    F    N

7. annus *(year)*            M    F    N

8. flumen *(river)*          M    F    N

9. porta *(gate)*            M    F    N

10. animus *(soul)*          M    F    N

# 3. WHAT IS MEANT BY NUMBER?

**Number** is the indication of a word as singular or plural. When a word refers to one person or thing, it is said to be **singular;** when it refers to more than one, it is called **plural.**

Here is a list of parts of speech that have number:

| English | Latin |
|---------|-------|
| nouns | nouns |
| verbs | verbs |
| pronouns | pronouns |
| demonstrative adjectives | adjectives |

The plural of a word is formed according to different rules, depending on the part of speech to which it belongs. In this section let us explain the plural of nouns (see **What is a Noun?**, p. 4).

**IN ENGLISH**
A plural noun is usually spelled differently and pronounced differently from the singular. A singular noun is made plural in several ways:

■ by adding an **-s** or **-es**

> book → books
> kiss → kisses

■ by making a spelling change or addition

> man → men
> mouse → mice
> leaf → leaves
> child → children

Some nouns, called **collective nouns,** refer to a group of persons or things, but they are considered singular.

> A football *team* has eleven players.
> The *family* is all here now.
> The *crowd* was under control.

**IN LATIN**

A singular noun is usually made plural by having its ending changed, although there are words that change internally as well.

- most singular feminine nouns change the ending -a to -ae

| alumna | → | alumnae | *graduate* | → | *graduates (female)* |
| puella | → | puellae | *girl* | → | *girls* |

- most masculine nouns change the ending **-us** to **-ī**

| amīcus | → | amīcī | *friend* | → | *friends* |
| alumnus | → | alumnī | *graduate* → | *graduates (male)* |

- most neuter nouns change the ending **-um** to **-a**

| medium | → | media |
| datum | → | data |

- a few words that end in **-ex** or **-ix** change to **-icēs**

| index | → | indicēs |
| appendix | → | appendicēs |

▼▼▼▼▼▼▼▼▼▼▼▼▼▼REVIEW ▼▼▼▼▼▼▼▼▼▼▼▼▼▼▼

Using the ending changes listed above, write the equivalent plural form of the Latin nouns below.

1. alumna        _____

2. alumnus       _____

3. annus         _____

4. templum       _____

5. littera       _____

6. curriculum    _____

7. porta         _____

8. animus        _____

9. rosa          _____

10. index        _____

## 4. WHAT ARE DEFINITE AND INDEFINITE ARTICLES?

An **article** is a word which is placed before a noun to show if the noun refers to a particlular person, place, thing, animal or idea, or if the noun refers to an unspecified person, place, thing, animal or idea. Since it modifies a noun, the article is considered an adjective.

**IN ENGLISH**
The definite article *the* is placed before the noun if it refers to a specific person, place, thing, animal, or idea.

> I saw *the* boy who took *the* apple.
>        |                    |
>   specific boy        specific apple

The indefinite article *a* or *an* is placed before the noun to show that the noun does not refer to a particular person, place, thing, animal, or idea.

- *a* is used before a word beginning with a consonant

> I saw *a* boy in the house.
>        |
>   not a particular boy

- *an*  is used before a word beginning with a vowel

> I ate *an* apple.
>        |
>   not a particular apple

**IN LATIN**
There are no articles. When a Latin sentence is translated into English, the articles must be added, if necessary. Your knowledge of English and the meaning of the sentence will help you supply the correct article *(a, an, or the)* or you may omit the article entirely.

> Puella in casā habitat.
> girl    in house  lives
> *The girl lives in a house.*

> Milﾖtēs nōn semper sunt fortēs.
> soldier  not  always  are  brave
> *Soldiers are not always brave.*

▼▼▼▼▼▼▼▼▼▼▼▼▼▼REVIEW ▼▼▼▼▼▼▼▼▼▼▼▼▼▼▼▼

Below are word-for-word translations of Latin sentences into English. Write the complete English sentence, changing the word order and adding the appropriate articles, *a, an,* or *the* where necessary.

1. Puer in silvīs habitat.
    boy   in  woods lives

_____

2. Casam nōn habet.
    house   not   he does have

_____

3. Animālia fera eum cūrant.
    animals    wild  him   take care of

_____

## 5. WHAT IS MEANT BY CASE?

**Case** is the change in the form of a word to show how it functions within a sentence. This change of form usually takes place in the ending of the word; sometimes, however, the entire word changes.

### IN ENGLISH
The order of words in a sentence signals the function of the nouns and hence shows the meaning of the whole sentence. We easily recognize the difference in meaning between the following two sentences purely on the basis of word order. The nouns themselves remain the same even though they serve different functions in each sentence.

> The girl sees the bull on the shore.
> Here *the girl* is seeing, and *the bull* is what she sees.

> The bull sees the girl on the shore.
> Here *the bull* is seeing, and *the girl* is whom it sees.

The words for *girl* and *bull* are spelled the same whatever their function in the sentence. It is the word order that indicates the meaning of the sentence.

In English, there are three cases:

1. The **nominative case** or **subjective case** is used for the person or thing doing the action of the verb: *girl* in the first sentence because she is doing the seeing; *bull* in the second sentence because he is doing the seeing.

   The nominative case is used for words which function as subjects (see **What is a Subject?**, p. 22) and predicate words (see **What is a Predicate Word?**, p. 25).

2. The **objective case** is used for the person or thing receiving the action of the verb: *bull* in the first sentence because it is what the girl sees; *girl* in the second sentence because she is what the bull sees. In English the words are spelled the same in the nominative and objective cases.

   The objective case is used for words which function as direct objects, indirect objects, and objects of prepositions (see **What are Objects?**, p. 29).

3. The **possessive case** is used to indicate ownership.

> The girl sees the *farmer's* bull on the shore.
> The *farmer* is the person who owns the bull, and the ownership is indicated by 's added to the *farmer*.

As you can see from the above examples, the form of the noun changes only when it is in the possessive case *(farmer* becomes *farmer's)*.

Besides nouns showing possession with 's, in English we can see change of case also with pronouns (see **What is a Personal Pronoun?**, p. 37). In the examples below, it is not just the word order but also the form, i.e. the case, of the pronoun which affects the meaning of the sentence.

> *I* know *them.*
> subjective objective

> *They* know *me.*
> subjective objective

We do not say, "*I* know *they* " or "*They* know *I* " because the forms "they" and "I" cannot be used as objects of a verb (see **What are Objects?**, p. 29). If you can recognize the different cases of pronouns in English, you may find it easier to understand the Latin case system.

**IN LATIN**
Word order alone rarely shows the function of nouns within a sentence. Instead, the different endings of the Latin nouns indicate the changes called case. As long as the nouns are put in their proper case, the words in the sentence can be moved around in a variety of ways without changing the essential meaning of the sentence.

Look at the three ways the following sentence can be expressed in Latin:

> *The girl sees the bull on the shore.*[1]

> Puella taurum in rīpā videt.
> girl    bull    on shore  sees

> Taurum in rīpā puella videt.
> bull    on shore  girl    sees

> In rīpā taurum puella videt.
> on shore  bull    girl    sees

[1]The god Jupiter fell in love with the maiden Europa and came to earth in the form of a bull. After the bull had enticed the girl onto his back, he travelled across the sea with her to Crete.

The endings of the words (highlighted in the above example) show the case and function of the words in the sentence: "puella" must be the subject and "taurum"must be the object. This makes it evident that the *girl* is doing the looking and the *bull* is what she sees. Putting a word in the first position, i.e., at the beginning of the sentence, merely serves to emphasize that word. For instance, when **puella** *(girl)* is in the first position, it means that the girl and not someone else is seeing the bull; when **taurum** *(bull)* is in the first position it means that the girl sees the bull and not some other creature; when **in rīpā** *(on the shore)* is in the first position, it means that the girl sees the bull on the shore and not somewhere else.

Latin nouns, pronouns and adjectives have five main cases, each reflecting a different function of the word in a sentence. Each case also has a singular and a plural form (see **What is Meant by Number?, p. 9**). All these possible forms are called a declension. When you memorize a declension, the cases are usually in the following sequence:

1. The **nominative case**—This is the form listed in a vocabulary list or dictionary. It is the case used for the subject of a sentence and for predicate words (see **What is a Subject?**, p .22, and **What is a Predicate Word?**, p. 25).

    The *girl* looks at the bull.
    subject —→ **puella** nominative case in Latin

    Jupiter is a *god*.
    predicate word —→ **deus** nominative case in Latin

2. The **genitive case**—This form is used to show possession (see **What is the Possessive?**, p. 27).

    *Cupid's* arrows are sharp.
    possessor —→ **Cupidinis** genitive case in Latin

3. The **dative case**—This form is used for indirect objects (see p. 31 in **What are Objects?**).

    The girl gave flowers to the *bull*.
    indirect object —→ **taurō** dative case in Latin

4. The **accusative case**—This form is used for most direct objects and for objects of certain prepositions (see p. 30 in **What are Objects?**, and p. 167 in **What is a Preposition?**).

The bull saw the *girl.*
|
direct object ⟶ **puellam** accusative case in Latin

5. The **ablative case**—This form is used for objects of certain prepositions (see p. 32 in **What are Objects?**).

Jupiter is walking with *Mercury.*
|
object of preposition **cum** *(with)* ⟶ **Mercuriō** ablative case in Latin

The following two cases are usually omitted from declensions because
they generally use forms from other cases.

6. The **vocative case**—This form is used for the person or persons
being spoken to.

*Europa,* beware of the bull!
|
person being spoken to ⟶ **Eurōpa** vocative case in Latin

7. The **locative case**—This is the form used for the noun indicating the
location of someone or something (see p. 168 in **What is a Preposition?**).

Europa lived *at home* with her father.
|
location ⟶ **domi** locative case in Latin

You will have to memorize the case forms for all nouns, pronouns, and
adjectives. Fortunately, this is made easy by the Latin system of
declensions.

### The Declensions

Latin nouns are divided into five main groups called: the **first declension,** the **second declension,** the **third declension,** the **fourth declension,** and the **fifth declension**; hereafter indicated as 1st, 2nd, 3rd, 4th,
and 5th. Each declension has a different set of endings to reflect case.
You should memorize one sample for each declension, and that pattern
can then be applied to all other words in the same group or declension.

When you learn a new noun, it will usually be introduced in its nominative singular form. You must also memorize its genitive singular
form because that form gives you two essentials:

1. The ending helps you to identify the declension to which the word belongs.

| Declension | Genitive singular ending | Nominative | Genitive singular | |
|---|---|---|---|---|
| 1st | -ae | silva | silvae | *forest* |
| 2nd | -ī | animus | animī | *soul* |
| 3rd | -is | rēx | rēgis | *king* |
| 4th | -ūs | exercitus | exercitūs | *army* |
| 5th | -eī | fidēs | fideī | *faith* |

2. The genitive singular minus the ending gives you the stem to which the case endings of each declension are attached. To find this stem, merely drop the genitive ending from the genitive singular form.

| Declension | Genitive singular | Stem | |
|---|---|---|---|
| 1st | silvae | silv- | *forest* |
| 2nd | animī | anim- | *soul* |
| 3rd | rēgis | rēg- | *king* |
| 4th | exercitūs | exercit- | *army* |
| 5th | fideī | fid- | *faith* |

The English derivatives of many Latin nouns are often based on the genitive singular stems and should help you remember the form.

| Nominative singular | | Genitive singular | English derivative |
|---|---|---|---|
| nōmen | *name* | nōminis | *nominate* |
| rēx | *king* | rēgis | *regal* |
| virgo | *maiden* | virginis | *virgin, virginal* |

Your Latin textbook will give you the endings which are to be added to the stems for each declension. Be sure to memorize those patterns. There are a few nouns that are irregular in that they do not follow a specific declension. Your textbook will identify them and you will have to learn them individually.

Since the learning of declensions is important for a beginning Latin student, let us go over an example of a noun of the first declension to see how the various cases are formed. The principle will be the same for any word that is declined, whatever the declension.

A vocabulary list or dictionary will list a noun as follows:

**silva, -ae,** *f., forest*

The first form is the nominative singular; the second form, -ae, is that noun's genitive singular ending; the f. stands for the gender; and the last word is the English equivalent. These are the steps to follow to establish how that noun is declined.

1. DECLENSION—Identify the declension by the second form listed.

   The genitive ending "-ae" tells you that it is a noun of the 1st declension and that you will have to add the case endings of that declension.

2. GENDER—Identify the gender.

   The "*f.*" tells you that it is a feminine noun. Some declensions have two or three different sets of endings depending on whether the noun is masculine, feminine or neuter. You must establish the gender of the noun so that you will choose from the correct set of endings.

3. STEM—Find the stem by taking the genitive singular form and dropping the ending.

   silv-ae
       |   |
   stem ending

4. ENDING—Add the endings of the first declension listed below.

| | Case | Singular | Plural |
|---|---|---|---|
| | nominative | -a | -ae |
| | genitive | -ae | -ārum |
| IO | dative | -ae | -īs |
| DO | accusative | -am | -ās |
| | ablative | -ā | -īs |

Thus, the entire declension of the word **silva** reads as follows:

| Case | Singular | Plural | Usage |
|---|---|---|---|
| nominative | silva | silvae | *subject or predicate word* |
| genitive | silvae | silvārum | *possession* |
| dative | silvae | silvīs | *indirect object* |
| accusative | silvam | silvās | *direct object* |
| | | | *or object of preposition* |
| ablative | silvā | silvīs | *object of preposition* |
| | | | *or adverbial expressions* |

Notice that the -ā of the ablative singular ending has a long mark called a **macron** over it, indicating that it is a long vowel. It is important to mark the long -ā of the ablative singular to differentiate it from the short -a of the nominative singular ending.[1]

You can apply this same pattern for all the nouns of the first declension and for first declension feminine adjectives modifying them. If you are dealing with a noun of another declension, follow the same procedure, adding the appropriate endings.

### Choosing the Proper Noun Form

To choose the proper form of a Latin noun in a sentence, you will have to consider the following : its function, its case, its declension, its gender and its number.

Here is a series of steps you should follow for a sample sentence:

> The girls give the bull flowers.

1. FUNCTION—Determine how each noun functions in the sentence (see **What is a Subject?,** p. 22 and **What are Objects?,** p. 29).

| girls | → | subject |
| bull | → | indirect object |
| flowers | → | direct object |

2. CASE—Determine what case corresponds to the function you have identified in step 1.

| girls | → | subject | → | nominative case |
| bull | → | indirect object | → | dative case |
| flowers | → | direct object | → | accusative case |

3. DECLENSION—Identify the declension of each Latin noun based on the ending of the genitive singular.

| | | **Genitive** | | |
| girls | → | puellae | → | 1st declension |
| bull | → | taurī | → | 2nd declension |
| flowers | → | flōris | → | 3rd declension |

---

[1]Vowels in Latin are either long or short. The long ones are marked with the macron or long mark, indicating the length of time they are held and how they are pronounced. Refer to your Latin textbook for the rules.

4. GENDER—Establish the gender of each noun based on the indication in the dictionary (see **What is Meant by Gender?,** p. 6).

| girl | → | puella, *f.* | → | feminine |
|------|---|--------------|---|-----------|
| bull | → | taurus, *m.* | → | masculine |
| flower | → | flōs, *m.* | → | masculine |

5. NUMBER—Establish the number of each noun (see **What is Meant by Number?,** p. 9).

| girls | → | plural |
|-------|---|--------|
| bull | → | singular |
| flowers | → | plural |

6. SELECTION—Choose the proper form for each noun based on each noun's declension, case, gender, and number.

Puellae taurō flōrēs dant.

| 1st. | 2nd. | 3rd. |
|------|------|------|
| nom. | dat. | acc. |
| fem. | masc. | masc. |
| pl. | sing. | pl. |

Notice how changing the function of a word in a Latin sentence requires changing its case and form as well.

*The bull gives the girls flowers.*
Taurus puellīs flōrēs dat.

| nom. | dat. | acc. |
|------|------|------|
| masc. | fem. | masc. |
| sing. | pl. | pl. |

## Nota Bene

The above is only an introduction to the concept of case. Your Latin textbook will go over all the cases and their various uses in detail.

▼▼▼▼▼▼▼▼▼▼▼▼▼▼▼▼REVIEW ▼▼▼▼▼▼▼▼▼▼▼▼▼▼▼▼▼

Circle the case that you would use in Latin for the nouns in the sentences below: nominative (N), genitive (G), dative (D), accusative (Acc), or ablative (ABL).

1. The bull carried off Europa to Crete.

| bull | → subject | N | G | D | Acc | ABL |
|---|---|---|---|---|---|---|
| Europa | → direct object | N | G | D | Acc | ABL |
| Crete | → object of preposition **ad** + Acc | N | G | D | Acc | ABL |

2. On the island, Europa produced a son.

| island | → object of preposition **in** + Abl | N | G | D | Acc | ABL |
|---|---|---|---|---|---|---|
| Europa | → subject | N | G | D | Acc | ABL |
| son | → direct object | N | G | D | Acc | ABL |

3. The name of the son was Minos, and he gave his name to the kings of Crete.

| name | → subject | N | G | D | Acc | ABL |
|---|---|---|---|---|---|---|
| son | → possessive | N | G | D | Acc | ABL |
| Minos | → predicate word | N | G | D | Acc | ABL |
| name | → direct object | N | G | D | Acc | ABL |
| kings | → indirect object | N | G | D | Acc | ABL |
| Crete | → possessive | N | G | D | Acc | ABL |

# 6. WHAT IS A SUBJECT?

The **subject** of a sentence is the person or thing that performs the action of the verb.[1] When you wish to find the subject of a sentence, always look for the verb first; then ask, *who?* or *what?* before the verb. The answer will be the subject.

**IN ENGLISH**

The subject of the sentence performs the action of the verb. Subject words are often referred to as being in the **subjective case** (see p. 13).

> The goddess talks to the woman.
> *Who* talks to the woman? Answer: the goddess.
> *The goddess* is the singular subject.
>
> Apollo and Diana are the children of the goddess.
> *Who* are the children of the goddess? Answer: Apollo and Diana.
> *Apollo and Diana* is the plural subject.

Train yourself to ask "who" or "what" to find the subject. Never assume that a word is the subject because it comes first in the sentence. Subjects can be in many different places of a sentence, as you can see in the following examples in which the subject is in **boldface** and the verb is *italicized.*

> After listening to his mother, **Apollo** *killed* the sons of the queen.[2]
> Did **Apollo** *kill* all the sons of the queen?
> Grieving the loss of her children, all alone *stood* **Niobe.**

Some sentences have more than one main verb; you have to find the subject of each verb.

> **Latona** *calls* her children, and **they** *kill* the children of Niobe.
> **Latona** is the singular subject of the first verb, *calls.*
> **They** is the plural subject of the second verb, *kill.*

A singular subject takes a singular verb; a plural subject takes a plural verb. The verb must agree with its subject in number (see **What is Meant by Number?**, p. 9).

---

[1] The subject performs the action in the active sentence, but is acted upon in a passive sentence (see **What is Meant by Active and Passive Voice?**, p. 84).

[2] Niobe had boasted about her seven sons and seven daughters, asking the women of the town to pray to her and not to the goddess Latona, who only had one son and daughter, Apollo and Diana. The goddess, enraged, sent her powerful children to kill the sons and daughters of Niobe.

**IN LATIN**

It is particularly important that you recognize the subject of a sentence so that you will put it in the proper case (see **What is Meant by Case?**, p. 13). The subject of a Latin sentence is in the nominative case.

>*Jupiter loves Europa.*
>    *Who* loves Europa? Answer: Jupiter.
>**Iuppiter** Eurōpam amat.
>
>nominative masculine
>singular

>*The nymphs like the beautiful picture.*
>    *Who* likes the beautiful picture? Answer: the nymphs.
>**Nymphae** pictūram pulchram amant.
>
>nominative feminine
>plural

>*Beautiful gifts are pleasing to the goddess.*
>    *What* is pleasing to the goddess? Answer: gifts.
>**Dōna** pulchra sunt deae grāta.
>
>nominative neuter
>plural

## *Nota Bene*

In both English and Latin it is very important to find the subject of each verb. Not only does each subject have to be in the nominative, but you must make sure that each verb agrees with its subject; that is, you must use a singular verb with a singular subject, and a plural verb with a plural subject (see **What is a Verb Conjugation?**, p. 53).

▼▼▼▼▼▼▼▼▼▼▼▼▼▼▼▼▼REVIEW ▼▼▼▼▼▼▼▼▼▼▼▼▼▼▼▼▼

Find the subjects in the sentences below.

- Next to Q, write the question you need to ask to find the subject.
- Next to A, write the answer, i.e., the subject.
- Circle if the subject is singular (S) or plural (P).

1. Vesta is the goddess of the sacred fire in Rome.

Q: _____

A: _____    S        P

2. The Vestal Virgins tend the sacred fire.

Q: _____

A: _____    S        P

3. In the Forum stands the round temple of Vesta.

Q: _____

A: _____    S        P

# 7. WHAT IS A PREDICATE WORD?

A **predicate word** is a word which defines or describes the sentence's subject to which it is connected by a linking verb. A **linking verb** is a verb which connects or *links* a noun, pronoun, or adjective back to the subject.

## IN ENGLISH

The nouns, pronouns or adjectives following linking verbs are considered predicate words. Some common linking verbs in English are forms of the verbs *to be, to seem, to appear, to become.* (A linking verb is almost like an equal sign: "Mark is my best friend." Mark = my best friend.)

Arachne is a foolish *girl.*[1]  [Arachne = girl]

        linking
        verb
subject        predicate noun

Foolish men are *those* who challenge the gods.

        linking
        verb
   subject     predicate pronoun

Minerva becomes *angry.*

        linking
        verb
  subject      predicate adjective

## IN LATIN

Predicate words are in the same case as the subject, namely the nominative. Learn to recognize the various forms of linking verbs such as **esse** *(to be)*, **fierī** *(to become)*, and **vidērī** *(to seem),* so that you can identify the words which follow as predicate words and put them in the nominative case.

Arachnē est **puella** stulta.

        linking
        verb
subject      predicate noun
   └nom. fem. sing.┘

*Arachne is a foolish girl.*

---

[1]Arachne was a skillful weaver who challenged the goddess Minerva to a weaving contest. The goddess, enraged that the girl was so presumptuous, changed her into a spider.

Hominēs stultī sunt **illī** quī deōs prōvocant.

```
                    |
               linking
                verb
subject                    predicate pronoun
     └─ nom. masc. pl. ─┘
```

*Foolish men are **those** who challenge the gods.*

Minerva fit **īrāta.**

```
                |
           linking
            verb
subject         predicate adjective
└─nom. fem. sing.─┘
```

*Minerva becomes **angry.***

## Nota Bene

In order to choose the proper case in Latin, it is important that you do not confuse predicate words with objects (see **What are Objects?**, p. 29).

▼▼▼▼▼▼▼▼▼▼▼▼▼▼REVIEW ▼▼▼▼▼▼▼▼▼▼▼▼▼▼▼

Circle the linking verb in the sentences below.

▪ Draw an arrow from the predicate word back to the subject.

1. The goddesses are angry.

2. Apollo is a proud god.

3. Daphne is the daughter of a river god.

4. It is he who loves the girl.

5. These are the enemies whom you fear.

## 8. WHAT IS THE POSSESSIVE?

The term **possessive** means that one noun, i.e., the possessor, owns or *possesses* another noun, i.e., the possessed.

the teacher's book
noun    noun
possessor possessed

**IN ENGLISH**
You can show possession in one of two ways:

1. with an apostrophe

- by adding an apostrophe + "s" to a singular possessor noun

  the *teacher's* book
  *Ovid's* poetry
  the *bird's* song

- by adding an apostrophe to the plural possessor noun

  the *girls'* father
  the *boys'* mother

2. with the word "of" followed by the possessor noun

   the book *of the teacher*
   the poetry *of Ovid*
   the song *of the bird*

**IN LATIN**
Possession is shown by using the genitive case for the possessor, the noun that owns the other noun. There is no Latin word for "of" in the sense of possession.

liber **magistrī**
nom.  possessor
        genitive sing.
*the book **of the teacher** (or **the teacher's** book)*

pater **puellārum**
nom.  possessors
        genitive pl.
*the father **of the girls** (or **the girls' father**)*

## Nota Bene

Not every use of the word "of" in English implies possession. "Of" also appears when one noun modifies another noun: *a ship of this kind, a wall of a hundred feet,* etc. Latin uses the genitive case for these "of" ideas:

puer **decem annorum**
*a boy of ten years*

Latin also uses the genitive for an object which is called the **objective genitive.**

Amōrem **pecūniae** dēmōnstrābat.
genitive sing.
*He showed a love of money.*

Odium **meī** erat manifestum.
genitive sing.
*His hatred of me was clear.*

▼▼▼▼▼▼▼▼▼▼▼▼▼▼▼REVIEW ▼▼▼▼▼▼▼▼▼▼▼▼▼▼▼▼

In the sentences below, underline the word or words for which you would use the genitive case in Latin.

- Circle whether the genitive is a possessive genitive (PG) or an objective genitive (OG).

1. Arachne's skill as a weaver was clear.          PG      OG

2. The foolish girl would not acknowledge the
   superior skill of Minerva.                       PG      OG

3. Arachne showed her love of weaving
   in a contest.                                    PG      OG

4. Arachne wove a tapestry about the
   evil deeds of the gods.                          PG      OG

# 9. WHAT ARE OBJECTS?

**Objects** are nouns or pronouns that receive the action of verbs or that complete prepositional phrases. In order to be able to choose the correct case of nouns or pronouns, you must understand the difference between the various kinds of objects in both English and Latin.

Most sentences consist, at the very least, of a subject and a verb.

> Children play.
> Work stopped.

The subject of the sentence is a noun or a pronoun (see **What is a Subject?**, p. 22). Most sentences, however, contain other nouns or pronouns. Many of these function as objects. These objects are divided into three categories, depending on how they are related to the verb: direct objects, indirect objects, and objects of a preposition.

## Direct and Indirect Objects

**IN ENGLISH**

The terms "direct" and "indirect" indicate the manner in which the noun or pronoun object is related to the verb.

1. A **direct object** receives the action of the verb directly, without a preposition separating the verb from the receiver. It answers the one-word question *what?* or *whom?* asked after the verb.

> The god loves the **nymph.**
> > The god loves *whom?* Answer: The nymph.
> > *The nymph* is the direct object.

> The girl sees the **bull.**
> > The girl sees *what?* Answer: The bull.
> > *The bull* is the direct object.

Object words are often referred to as being in the objective case (see p. 13). Never assume that a word is the direct object. Always ask the one-word question, and if you do not get an answer, you do not have a direct object in the sentence. Some sentences do not have direct objects.

> The girls work well.
> > The girls work *whom?* No one, no answer possible.
> > The girls work *what?* Nothing, no answer possible.
> >
> > This sentence has no direct object. *Well* is an adverb telling how the girls worked.

2. An **Indirect object** also receives the action of the verb, but it receives the action indirectly, through the prepositions *"to"* or *"for."* It explains "to whom" or "for whom," or "to what" or "for what" the action of the verb is done. The *"to"* or *"for"* is usually expressed in the sentence; sometimes it is understood. An indirect object answers the two-word question *to whom?* or *for whom?* or *to what?* or *for what?* asked after the verb.[1]

> The boy gives a present *to his mother.*
> The boy gives his *mother* a present.
>> The boy gives *to whom?* Answer: To his mother.
>> His *mother* is the indirect object.

> The farmer did a favor *for me.*
> The farmer did *me* a favor.
>> The farmer did a favor *for whom?* Answer: For me.
>> *Me* is the indirect object.

In English, the only way to establish if a noun is a direct or indirect object is by asking a question to see how it is related to the verb.

**IN LATIN**
Direct and indirect objects are identified in the same way as they are in English. Unlike English, however, each function corresponds to a different case, so that the ending of the noun itself will reveal whether it is a direct or an indirect object.

1. **Direct objects**: Most English direct objects are in the accusative case in Latin.

> *The god loves the **girl**.*
>> The god loves *whom?* Answer: The girl.
>> *The girl* is the direct object.
> Deus **puellam** amat.
>> direct object ⟶ accusative

> *The girl sees the **bull**.*
>> The girl sees *what?* Answer: The bull.
>> *The bull* is the direct object.
> Puella **taurum** videt.
>> direct object ⟶ accusative

---

[1]Every use of *"to"* or *"for"* does not identify an indirect object. *To* and *for* can also introduce prepositional phrases: ad īnsulam *(to the island)* and prō vīnō *(for wine)* (see pp. 33, 166).

2. **Indirect objects**: English indirect objects are in the dative case in
Latin.

> *The boy gives **his mother** a gift.*
> *The boy gives a gift to **his mother**.*
>> The boy gives *to whom?* Answer: To his mother.
>> *His mother* is the indirect object.
>
> Puer **mātrī** dōnum dat.
>> indirect object —→ dative

> *Mark did **me** a favor.*
> *Mark did a favor for **me**.*
>> Mark did a favor *for whom?* Answer: For me.
>> *Me* is the indirect object.
>
> Marcus **mihi** grātum fēcit.
>> indirect object —→ dative

## *Nota Bene*

Although most Latin verbs take the accusative for the direct object
and the dative for the indirect object, some verbs take other cases.
Your Latin textbook will indicate these exceptions. Be sure that
you work with the case required in Latin.

### Sentences with a Direct and an Indirect Object

**IN ENGLISH**

When a sentence has two different objects, a direct and an indirect
object, there are two possible constructions:

1. subject (S) + verb (V) + indirect object (IO) + direct object (DO)

> He gave the goddess flowers.
> S     V        IO     DO
>
>> He gave *what?* Flowers.
>> *Flowers* is the direct object.
>
>> He gave flowers *to whom?* To the goddess.
>> *The goddess* is the indirect object.

2. the subject (S) + verb (V) + direct object (DO) + **to** + indirect
object (IO)

> He gave flowers to the goddess.
> S     V    DO             IO

The change of word order does not change the function of each word.

**IN LATIN**
The word order of a direct and indirect object in a sentence is not as important as are the case endings in Latin. Once you have determined which object is direct and which is indirect, just put the direct object in the accusative and the indirect object in the dative case. The ending of the word will reveal its function in the sentence.

> *He gave the **goddess flowers.***
>            indirect   direct
>            object     object

> **Deae flōrēs** dedit.    **Flōrēs deae** dedit.
> ind. obj.  dir. obj.     dir. obj.  ind. obj.
> dat.        acc.        acc.      dat.
> *(Goddess* emphasized.)  *(Flowers* emphasized.)

## Objects of a Preposition

**IN ENGLISH**
The noun or pronoun which follows a preposition other than *"to"* or *"for"* is called an **object of a preposition** (see **What is a Preposition?**, p. 166). The object of the preposition answers the two-word question made up of the preposition + *what?* or the preposition + *whom?*

> The tree is ***in the forest.***
> The tree is *in what?* Answer: In the forest.
> *Forest* is the object of the preposition *in.*

> Jupiter is walking ***with Mercury.***
> Jupiter is walking *with whom?* Answer: With Mercury.
> *Mercury* is the object of the preposition *with.*

There are many prepositions which take objects: *behind* the house, *out* the window, *without* him, *after* the war, *beside* the river, *before* the storm, *with* Diana, *inside* the palace, *over* the hill, *for* the emperor, *alongside* the road.

**IN LATIN**
Nouns and pronouns functioning as objects of a preposition are in the ablative or accusative case depending on the preposition. It is impor-

tant, therefore, that when you learn a new preposition you learn not only its meaning but also the case of the noun which follows it.

- **pro** *(before)* + ablative

    *The tree is **before the temple**.*
    The tree is *before what?* Before the temple.
    *Temple* is the object of the preposition *before*.

    Arbor est **prō templō.**
    |
    obj. of prep. **prō** + ablative

- **per** *(through)* + accusative

    *The bear wandered **through the forest**.*
    The bear wandered *through what?* Through the forest.
    *Woods* is the object of the preposition *through*.

    Ursa **per silvam** errābat.
    |
    obj. of prep. **per** + accusative

## Nota Bene

The relationship between a verb and its object is often different in English and Latin. For example, a verb may take an object of a preposition in English, but a direct object in Latin. Below is an example of two English verbs that are followed by a preposition and its object, while the equivalent Latin verbs simply take a direct object in the accusative case.

- to look at—**spectāre** + accusative

    *The girls **are looking at** the stars.*
    Puellae stellās **spectant.**
    |          |          |
    subject    |        verb
           direct object → accusative

    The meaning of the verb **spectant** is "look at" and **stellās**, "stars," is the direct object in the accusative case.

- to wait for—**exspectāre** + accusative

    *The farmers **were waiting for** help.*
    Agricolae auxilium **exspectābant.**
    |          |          |
    subject    |        verb
           direct object → accusative

    The meaning of the verb **exspectābant** is "were waiting for" and **auxilium,**"help," is the direct object in the accusative case.

▼▼▼▼▼▼▼▼▼▼▼▼▼▼▼REVIEW ▼▼▼▼▼▼▼▼▼▼▼▼▼▼▼▼▼▼

Underline the objects in the sentences below.
■ Next to Q, write the question you need to ask to find the object.
■ Next to A, write the answer to the question you just asked.
■ Circle the type of each object: direct object (DO), indirect object (IO), or
  object of a preposition (OP).

1. The king abandoned his daughter in the woods.

Q: _____

A: _____    DO    IO    OP

Q: _____

A: _____    DO    IO    OP

2. Wild animals raised Atalanta.

Q: _____

A: _____    DO    IO    OP

3. Atalanta, now grown, went to the palace.

Q: _____

A: _____    DO    IO    OP

4. The king gave Atalanta his blessing.

Q: _____

A: _____    DO    IO    OP

Q: _____

A: _____    DO    IO    OP

# 10. WHAT IS A PRONOUN?

A **pronoun** is a word used in place of one or more nouns. It may stand, therefore, for a person, place, thing, or idea.

For instance, instead of repeating the proper noun "Midas" in the following sentences, it is more desirable to use a pronoun in the second sentence.

> *Midas* likes gold. *Midas* turns everything to gold.
> *Midas* likes gold. *He* turns everything to gold.

A pronoun can only be used to refer to something (or someone) that has already been mentioned. The word that the pronoun replaces or refers to is called the **antecedent** of the pronoun. In the example above, the pronoun *he* refers to the proper noun *Midas*. *Midas* is the antecedent of the pronoun *he*.

**IN ENGLISH**

There are different types of pronouns. They are studied in separate sections of this handbook. Listed below are the most important categories and the section where they are discussed in detail.

**Personal pronouns** change in form in the different persons and according to the function they have in the sentence.

- as subject (see p. 22)

> *I* go; *they* read; *he* runs; *she* sings.

- as direct object (see p. 29)

> Midas loves *it*. Pan saw *her*. Apollo killed *them*.

- as indirect object (see p. 30)

> The goddess gave *him* advice.
> Send *them* help.
> Give *her* gifts.

- as object of a preposition (see pp. 32, 42-3)

> Come with *me*.
> This is a gift for *them*.
> The Lord be with *you*.

**Reflexive pronouns** refer back to the subject of the sentence (p. 22).

> He saw *himself* in the water.
> They freed *themselves* from danger.

**Interrogative pronouns** are used in questions at the beginning of the question sentence. They are the first words, unless they are objects of a preposition (see p. 145).

*Who* is coming?
*What* did the god say?
*Whom* did you see?
*To whom* did you give your letter?

**Demonstrative pronouns** are used to point out persons or things (see p. 157).

*This* is beautiful. *That* is ugly.
*These* can be planted now. *Those* are ruined.

**Possessive pronouns** are used to show possession (see p. 152).

Whose house is this? It is *mine.*
*Yours* is on the next street.

**Relative pronouns** are used to introduce relative subordinate clauses (see p. 159).

The god *who* came is powerful.
The goddess *whom* you worship is listening to your prayers.

**Indefinite pronouns** indicate certain people or things not clearly seen.

*Someone* is coming.
I can make out *something*.
*One* should be careful.

Since the indefinite pronouns in Latin correspond in usage to their English equivalents, there is no special section devoted to this type of pronoun. The various indefinite pronouns can be studied as vocabulary entries in your textbook.

**IN LATIN**
These different types of pronouns also exist in Latin. They are different from English pronouns in that Latin pronouns always reflect case, gender, and number. This handbook and your textbook will indicate to you the rules of agreement for the various types of pronouns.

## 11. WHAT IS A PERSONAL PRONOUN?

A **personal pronoun** is a word taking the place of a noun which refers to a person or a thing.

>*I* am very happy.
>*They* enjoy learning Latin.
>Please look at *me*.
>The nymph liked the flower and picked *it*.

In both English and Latin, personal pronouns have different forms to show the pronoun's function in the sentence; these forms are called **case forms** (see **What is Meant by Case?**, p. 13).

We will study the two types of pronouns separately: pronouns as subjects and pronouns as objects.

### Personal Pronouns used as Subjects

**IN ENGLISH**
Personal pronouns used as subjects are said to be in the **subjective** or **nominative case**. A different pronoun is used depending on the person referred to, *I* as opposed to *you,* and some pronouns such as *she* and *they* show whether one person or more than one person is involved.

>*She* ran, but *we* walked.
>>*Who* ran? Answer: She.
>>*She* is the singular subject of the verb *ran*.
>
>>*Who* walked? Answer: We.
>>*We* is the plural subject of the verb *walked*.

Here is a list of the of pronouns used as subject:

|  | Singular | Plural |
|---|---|---|
| 1st person | I | we |
| *the person (s) speaking* | | |
| 2nd person | you | you |
| *the person (s) spoken to* | | |
| 3rd person | | |
| *the person (s)* | he, she, it | they |
| *or thing(s) spoken about* | | |

**IN LATIN**
Pronouns used as subjects are in the nominative case (see **What is Meant by Case?**, p. 13).

| English | | Latin |
|---|---|---|
| I | 1st person singular<br>*the person speaking* | **ego** |
| you | 2nd person singular<br>*the person spoken to* | **tū** |
| he<br>she<br>it | 3rd person singular<br>*the person or thing*<br>*spoken about* | { **is** (masc.)<br>**ea** (fem.)<br>**id** (neut.) |
| we | 1st person plural<br>*the person speaking*<br>*+ others* | **nōs** |
| you | 2nd person plural<br>*the persons spoken to* | **vōs** |
| they | 3rd person plural<br>*the persons or things*<br>*spoken about* | { **eī** (masc.)<br>**eae** (fem.)<br>**ea** (neut.) |

Let us look more closely at the two subject pronouns: *you* and *it* which have more than one Latin form so that you can learn how to choose the correct one.

### "You" – The singular and plural forms
**IN ENGLISH**
There is no difference in form between "you" in the singular and "you" in the plural. For example, if there were many people in a room and you asked aloud, "Are *you* coming with me?," the "you" could stand for one person or for many.

**IN LATIN**
There is a difference between "you" in the singular and "you" in the plural.

> *You are the cause of my grief.*
> > *You* refers to one person.
> > Use singular **tū**.
> **Tū** es causa dolōris meī.

> *You all are friends.*
> > *You* refers to many people.
> > Use plural **vōs**.
> **Vōs** omnēs sunt amīcī.

## "IT" – The gender of the third person singular pronoun
### IN ENGLISH
The neuter pronoun "it" is used to replace the noun for any object or idea.

> My sword is precious. *It* saved my life.
> I love my country. *It* has good citizens.
> Where is that temple? *It* is in the city.

### IN LATIN
Since Latin nouns have gender (see **What is Meant by Gender?**, p. 6), the pronouns which replace them must also show gender. Thus a pronoun will be either masculine, feminine, or neuter depending on the gender of the noun to which it refers, its antecedent.

Follow these steps to choose the correct form of *it* (**is, ea,** or **id**):

1. ANTECEDENT – Find the noun *it* replaces.
2. GENDER – Determine the gender of the antecedent in Latin.
3. FUNCTION – Determine the function of *it* in the sentence.[1]
4. CASE – Choose the case which corresponds to the function found in step 3.
5. SELECTION – Choose the pronoun based on steps 2 and 4.

> *My sword is precious. **It** saved my life.*
>   1. Antecedent: sword (**gladius**)
>   2. Gender: **Gladius** is masculine.
>   3. Function: subject of *saved*
>   4. Case: nominative
>   5. Selection: **Is** masculine nominative
> Gladius meus est cārus. **Is** vītam meam servāvit.

> *I love my country. **It** has good citizens.*
>   1. Antecedent: country (**patriam**)
>   2. Gender: **Patriam** is feminine.
>   3. Function: subject of *has*
>   4. Case: nominative
>   5. Selection: **Ea** feminine singular
> Patriam amō. **Ea** cīvēs bonōs habet.

---

[1]Since this section is devoted to subject pronouns, *it* in all the examples is a subject. Do not forget *it* can also be an object (see pp. 35, 40-1).

*Where is that temple?* **It is in the city.**
   1. Antecedent: temple **(templum)**
   2. Gender: **Templum** is neuter.
   3. Function: subject of *is*
   4. Case: nominative
   5. Selection: **Id** neuter nominative
Ubi est illud templum? **Id** est in urbe.

Latin generally omits the pronouns as subjects, since the personal endings attached to the verb serve the same function (see **What is a Verb Conjugation?**, p. 53). Only when the subject pronoun is being stressed, or when the gender of a 3rd person singular subject needs to be indicated, would the Romans have included it.

   **Ego** sum amīcus tuus, non **ille.**
   *I am your friend, not **that man.***
      *I* is being stressed, as opposed to *that man.*

   Puer et puella mē spectant. **Ea** mē nōn amat.
   *The boy and girl are watching me. **She** does not like me.*
      **Ea** is stated so that it is clear that it is the girl,
      not the boy, who "does not like me."

### Personal Pronouns as Objects

**IN ENGLISH**
When pronouns are used as direct or indirect objects or as objects of prepositions, they are said to be in the **objective case** (see **What are Objects?**, p. 29).

   They invited *him* and *me.*
      They invited *whom?* Answer: Him and me.
      *Him* and *me* are the direct objects of invited.

   I gave *them* my best work.
      I gave *to whom?* Answer: To them.
      *To them* is the indirect object of *gave.*

   They are coming with *you* and *her.*
      They are coming *with whom?* Answer: With you and her.
      *You* and *her* are objects of preposition *with*

Most pronouns that occur as objects in a sentence are different from the ones used as subjects. Compare the nominative and objective cases in English for the personal pronouns:

| Nominative | Objective |
|---|---|
| I | me |
| you | you |
| he, she, it | him, her, it |
| we | us |
| you | you |
| they | them |

Only *you* and *it* have the same form as subjects and as objects.

**IN LATIN**
Instead of a single objective case as in English, Latin has four cases of pronouns which are used as pronoun objects: the genitive, the dative, the accusative, and the ablative. The use of these different cases corresponds to the use of the same cases of nouns (see **What is Meant by Case?**, p. 13). The forms for the personal pronouns corresponding to the English object pronouns are as follows:

| Nominative Person | | OBJECTS | | | |
|---|---|---|---|---|---|
| | | Genitive[1] | Dative | Accusative | Ablative |
| | | | Singular | | |
| 1 | ego | meī | mihi | mē | mē |
| 2 | tu | tuī | tibi | tē | tē |
| 3 { *m.* | is | eius | eī | eum | eō |
| *f.* | ea | eius | eī | eam | eā |
| *n.* | id | eius | eī | id | eō |
| | | | Plural | | |
| 1 | nōs | nostrī | nōbīs | nōs | nōbīs |
| 2 | vōs | vestrī | vōbīs | vōs | vōbīs |
| 3 { *m.* | eī | eōrum | eīs | eōs | eīs |
| *f.* | eae | eārum | eīs | eās | eīs |
| *n.* | ea | eōrum | eīs | ea | eīs |

Remember that the Latin personal pronouns in the third person replace nouns having specific genders. (This has been discussed in detail for the third person in the nominative case on pp. 39-40.) Make sure that the gender of the pronoun is the same as the gender of the noun that it is replacing.

---

[1]This use of the genitive is an objective genitive use described on p. 28.

## Summary

In deciding which form of a personal pronoun to use in a Latin sentence, you will need to ask yourself the following questions:

1. PERSON—To which person does the pronoun refer (1st, 2nd, or 3rd, singular or plural)?

2. GENDER—In 3rd person, what is the gender of the pronoun or antecedent?

3. FUNCTION—What is the pronoun's function in the sentence?

4. CASE—What case in Latin is required for that particular function of the pronoun?

5. SELECTION—Choose the proper form (case, gender, and number) according to steps 1-4.

> *They live in the city.*
> 1. Person: 3rd person plural
> 2. Gender: Unknown - masculine or feminine
> 3. Function: subject
> 4. Case: nominative
> 5. Selection: **eī** (if *they* refers to men or men and women) or **eae** (if *they* refers to women)

**Eī** in urbe habitant.
**Eae** in urbe habitant.

> *We see **him**.*
> 1. Person: 3rd person singular
> 2. Gender: masculine
> 3. Function: direct object
> 4. Case: accusative
> 5. Selection: **eum**

**Eum** vidēmus.

> *We gave **her** a letter.*
> 1. Person: 3rd person singular
> 2. Gender: feminine
> 3. Function: indirect object
> 4. Case: dative
> 5. Selection: **eī**

Epistulam **eī** dedimus.

*They were writing about us.*
  1. Person: 1st person plural
  2. Gender: masculine and feminine (same form)
  3. Function: object of preposition *about*
  4. Case: ablative
  5. Selection: **nōbis** (preposition **dē** + ablative)
Dē **nōbis** scribēbant.

*The Lord be with you.*
  1. Person: 2rd person singular or plural
  2. Gender: masculine and feminine (same form)
  3. Function: object of preposition *with*
  4. Case: ablative (preposition **cum** + ablative)
  5. Selection: **vōbīs** (plural) or **tē** (singular)
Dominus **vōbīscum.**
Dominus **tēcum.**
  **Cum** is usually attached at the end of its pronoun object to form a single word.

▼▼▼▼▼▼▼▼▼▼▼▼▼▼▼REVIEW ▼▼▼▼▼▼▼▼▼▼▼▼▼▼▼▼▼

I. Using the chart on p. 38, write the Latin subject and object pronouns you would use to replace the words in **boldface.**

1. Children, **you** must all see the temple.         _____

2. Mars and Venus, **they** are the gods of Rome.     _____

3. **We** must all lay down our arms.                 _____

4. Venus helped **them** (the women).                 _____

5. The gods do not love **her.**                      _____

II. Determine the appropriate gender, number, and case for the Latin equivalent of *it* and *they.*

1. The gate is open. Please close *it.*

**Porta** *(gate)* is feminine.

GENDER:_____        NUMBER: _____        CASE: _____

2. My books are always ready. *They* are in my briefcase.

**Librī** *(books)* is masculine.

GENDER:_____        NUMBER: _____        CASE: _____

3. The gift of the gods is love. Take *it*!

**Dōnum** *(gift)* is neuter.

GENDER:_____        NUMBER: _____        CASE: _____

# 12. WHAT IS A VERB?

A **verb** is a word that expresses an action, state, or condition. The action can be physical, as in such verbs as *run, walk, climb, sing,* or mental, as in such verbs as *dream, think, believe,* and *hope.* Verbs like *be* and *become* express a state or condition rather than an action.

The verb is one of the most important words in a sentence; you usually cannot express a complete thought without a verb.

To help you learn to recognize verbs, here is a paragraph where the verbs are in italics. Some of the verbs are single words, and some are **verb phrases**, that is groups of words that make up a single verb idea.

> The myth about Jupiter who *came* to earth in the form of a human being *is* familiar to many people. Jupiter, king of the gods, *decided to test*[1] the hospitality of the people in a certain village. He *had taken* his son Mercury with him, and when the two *had entered* the village and *had sought* refuge for the night in many homes, every home *was closed* to them. The villagers *stoned* the strangers and *set* their dogs on them. Only the old Philemon and his wife Baucis *welcomed* the strangers in their humble cottage. Although they *thought* that the strangers *were* poor wanderers, they *set* their best table for them. *To thank*[1] the old couple, Jupiter *transformed* their cottage into a temple and *made* Philemon and Baucis custodians. At their death they *were* both *turned* into trees.

## IN ENGLISH

There are two kinds of verbs depending on whether or not the verb can take a direct object: transitive verbs and intransitive verbs.

A **transitive verb** is a verb which takes a direct object (see **What are Objects?**, p. 29). It is indicated by the abbreviation *v.t.* (verb transitive) in the dictionary.

> The old couple *welcomed* the strangers.
>        transitive verb    direct object

> The gods *changed* the cottage into a temple.
>     transitive verb   direct object

---

[1]Infinitive, see p. 50.

An **Intransitive verb** is a verb that does not take a direct object. It is indicated in the dictionary by the abbreviation *v.i.* (verb intransitive).

Philemon and Baucis *were* kind to the gods.
                   intransitive verb (no direct object)

The trees still *stand* on either side of the entrance.
          intransitive verb (no direct object)

Many verbs can be used both transitively and intransitively, depending on whether or not they have a direct object in the sentence.

The gods *entered* the house.
         transitive verb   direct object

The gods *entered*.
    intransitive verb (no direct object)

## IN LATIN
Verbs are identified in the same way in Latin as in English.

▼▼▼▼▼▼▼▼▼▼▼▼▼▼▼REVIEW ▼▼▼▼▼▼▼▼▼▼▼▼▼▼▼▼▼

Underline the verbs in the sentences below.
▪ Circle whether the verb is transitive (V.T.) or intranstive (V.I.)

1. Niobe praises her children.           V.T.    V.I.

2. Juno is watching her husband.       V.T.    V.I.

3. Daphne was running fast.          V.T.    V.I.

4. Jupiter loved many females.        V.T.    V.I.

5. Diana will kill all of Niobe's daugthers.    V.T.    V.I.

## 13. WHAT ARE THE PRINCIPAL PARTS OF A VERB?

The **principal parts** of a verb are those forms which we need to know in order to form all the different tenses.

**IN ENGLISH**

If we know the infinitive, the past tense, and the past participle of any verb, we can apply regular rules to form all the other tenses of that verb. These three forms constitute the principal parts of an English verb.

For example, in order to form the six main tenses of the verb *to eat*, we need to know *eat* (the form used in the infinitive *to eat*), *ate* (simple past), and *eaten* (past participle).

| | | | |
|---|---|---|---|
| **present** | I eat | **present perfect** | I have eaten |
| **past** | I ate | **past perfect** | I had eaten |
| **future** | I shall eat | **future perfect** | I shall have eaten |

The principal parts of a verb are either regular or irregular.

**Regular verbs** form their past tense and their past participle very predictably with the dictionary form of the verb + *-ed, -d* or *-t.* Since the past tense and the past participle of regular verbs are identical, these verbs really have only two principal parts, the infinitive and the past tense form.

| Infinitive | Past tense | Past Participle |
|---|---|---|
| to walk | walked | walked |
| to seem | seemed | seemed |
| to burn | burned | burned |
| | or burnt | or burnt |

**Irregular verbs** have unpredictable principal parts. As we grow up, we learn these forms simply by hearing them.

| Infinitive | Past tense | Past Participle |
|---|---|---|
| to be | was | been |
| to sing | sang | sung |
| to go | went | gone |
| to draw | drew | drawn |
| to write | wrote | written |

**IN LATIN**

A verb has four principal parts: the first person singular of the present tense, the infinitive, the first person singular of the perfect, followed by the perfect passive participle.

| Present tense 1st pers. sing. | Infinitive | Perfect tense 1st pers. sing. | Perfect passive participle |
|---|---|---|---|
| amō | amāre | amāvī | amātum |
| *I love, am loving, do love* | *to love* | *I loved, have loved, did love* | *having been loved* |

In the vocabulary of your textbook and in the dictionary, Latin verbs are listed under the first person singular of the present tense. For example, the verb *to love* is listed under **amō** (*I love*). The entry gives the four principal parts listed as: **amō, -āre, -āvī, -ātum** with part of the stem or base (**am-**) understood to be continued for each form. It is important to learn the principal parts of a verb, since they enable you to form the different tenses.

Many verbs are regular and you will only have to learn one pattern of principal parts which you can then apply to other verbs of the same group. Some verbs are irregular and the forms change completely; for example, **agō, agere, ēgī, actum** (*to do*). Irregular verbs will have to be memorized individually.

▼▼▼▼▼▼▼▼▼▼▼▼▼▼▼▼REVIEW ▼▼▼▼▼▼▼▼▼▼▼▼▼▼▼▼

I.Write the principal parts of these English verbs:

| Infinitive | Past Tense | Past Participle |
|---|---|---|
| 1. to think | _____ | _____ |
| 2. to run | _____ | _____ |
| 3. to drive | _____ | _____ |

II. Use **amŏ, amăre, amāvī, amātum** *(love)* as an example.

- On the first line provided, write the principal parts of the verb **laudō** *(praise)*.

- On the lines below, write the English translation of the principal parts above.

| | Present tense 1st pers. sing. | Infinitive | Perfect tense 1st pers. sing. | Perfect passive participle |
|---|---|---|---|---|
| LATIN: | _____ | _____ | _____ | _____ |
| ENGLISH: | _____ | _____ | _____ | _____ |
| | _____ | | _____ | |
| | _____ | | _____ | |

## 14. WHAT IS AN INFINITIVE?

An **Infinitive** is a form of a verb without person or number, giving its basic meaning.

**IN ENGLISH**

The infinitive is composed of two words, *to* + *verb*: *to love, to walk, to enjoy, to be*. When you look up a verb in a dictionary you find it without the *to*. This form is called the **dictionary form**: *love, walk, think, enjoy, be*.

All verbs have a present infinitive and a perfect infinitive. The **present infinitive** is usually *to* + the verb, or just the dictionary form of the verb. The **perfect infinitive** is *to have* + the past participle of the main verb.

| Present infinitive | Perfect infinitive |
|---|---|
| to be | to have been |
| to lead | to have led |
| to love | to have loved |

Verbs which can be used with passive meaning (see **What is Meant by Active and Passive Voice?**, p. 84) also have a present infinitive and a perfect infinitive for the passive voice. The **present passive infinitive** is formed with the the verb *to be* + the past participle of the main verb, and the **perfect passive infinitive** is formed with the phrase *to have been* + the past participle of the main verb.

| Present passive infinitive | Perfect passive infinitive |
|---|---|
| ("to be" does not have a passive) | |
| to be led | to have been led |
| to be loved | to have been loved |

The infinitive is generally used with another conjugated verb (see **What is a Verb Conjugation?**, p. 53).

*To learn* is challenging.
infinitive  conjugated verb

It is important *to be* on time.
conjugated verb    infinitive

Mark and Julia want *to come* home.

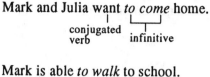

Mark is able *to walk* to school.

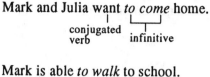

## IN LATIN

The present infinitive, the second principal part of the verb, ends in **-re.** It expresses in a single word the English two-word infinitive: *to sing* → **cantāre.**

As in English, Latin has a present infinitive and a perfect infinitive.

| **Present active infinitive** | **Perfect active infinitive** |
|---|---|
| amāre   *to love* | amāvisse   *to have loved* |

As in English, Latin verbs which can be used with passive meaning have a present and perfect infinitive form for the passive voice.

| **Present passive infinitive** | **Perfect passive infinitive** |
|---|---|
| amārī   *to be loved* | amātus, -a, -um esse *to have been loved* |

Your textbook will show you how to form these infinitives, as well as both active and passive future infinitives.

The present infinitive provides two essential verb elements:

1. CONJUGATION—The ending (**-āre, -ēre, -ere,** or **-īre**) enables you to identify the conjugation to which the verb belongs (see **What is a Verb Conjugation?**, p. 53).

2. PRESENT STEM—The stem of the present tense, called the **present stem,** gives you the stem to which the endings of the present, imperfect and future tenses are attached.

The main uses of the Latin infinitive are to complete the meaning of the conjugated verb, to function as a noun, and to be the verb in an indirect statement.

- as a complementary infinitive; i.e., to complete the meaning of another conjugated verb

> *Mark and Julia want **to come** home.*
> Marcus et Iūlia domum **venīre** dēsīderant.
>
> infinitive   conjugated verb

- as a noun, especially as subject of a sentence (see **What is a Subject?, pp. 22, 82**)

  *To learn is easy.*
  **Discere** est facile.
  |            |
  infinitive   conjugated verb

- in indirect statement (see **What is Meant by Direct and Indirect Statement?, p. 107**)

  *He says that the gods are coming.*
  |                          |___|
  verb of saying        verb in a subordinate "that" clause

  Dicit deōs **venīre.**
  |                |
  verb of saying   infinitive in indirect statement

▼▼▼▼▼▼▼▼▼▼▼▼▼▼REVIEW ▼▼▼▼▼▼▼▼▼▼▼▼▼▼▼▼

Write the active and passive infinitives for the following English verbs:

|              | ACTIVE | PASSIVE |
|--------------|--------|---------|
| 1. PRESENT:  | to eat | _____ |
| PERFECT:     | _____ | _____ |
| 2. PRESENT:  | to write | _____ |
| PERFECT:     | _____ | _____ |
| 3. PRESENT:  | to sing | _____ |
| PERFECT:     | _____ | _____ |

## 15. WHAT IS A VERB CONJUGATION?

A **verb conjugation** is a list of the six possible forms of the verb, one for each of the subject pronouns (1st, 2nd, 3rd persons, singular and plural) in a particular tense. The word *conjugation* comes from two Latin words: **con** *(with)* and **jug** *(join);* the idea is that endings are joined to the stem of the verb resulting in a verb form. In Latin grammar, the word *conjugation* is also used to refer to the four main patterns of Latin verbs according to their infinitive endings.

### IN ENGLISH
Verbs change very little. Let us look at the various forms of the verb **to love** in the present tense when each of the six possible personal pronouns is the performer of the action (see **What is a Personal Pronoun?**, p. 37).

**Person**

Singular

| | |
|---|---|
| 1st | *I love* the spring flowers. |
| 2nd | *You love* the spring flowers. |
| 3rd | *He loves* the spring flowers. |
| | *She loves* the spring flowers. |
| | *It loves* the spring flowers. |

Plural

| | |
|---|---|
| 1st | *We love* the spring flowers. |
| 2nd | *You love* the spring flowers. |
| 3rd | *They love* the spring flowers. |

Regular verbs change very little (see *love* or *loves* above), and in English you do not need "to conjugate" verbs. It is simpler to say that verbs take an "-s" in the third person singular of the present tense. The irregular verb *to be* has the most forms: I *am*, you *are*, he *is*, we *are*, you *are*, they *are*.

### IN LATIN
For each tense, a verb has six different endings, one for each person in the singular and in the plural. These endings are called **personal endings.**

Let us look at the same verb *to love*, **amāre**, conjugated in the present tense, to see the variety of personal endings:

| Person | Singular | Plural |
|--------|----------|--------|
| 1st | amō | amāmus |
| 2nd | amās | amātis |
| 3rd | amat | amant |

Since the personal endings indicate the subject, the subject pronoun usually does not have to be expressed; i.e., "amō" can only mean "*I love.*" In the third person singular, however, **amat** may mean "*he loves, she loves,*" or "*it loves,*" since the -t personal ending may refer to a masculine, feminine or neuter subject. You will have to look at previous sentences to find the subject. This previous information is called the **context**.

**Marcus** canem portat. Canem **amat**.
*Mark is carrying the dog. He loves the dog.*

**Iūlia** flōrēs portat. Flōrēs **amat**.
*Julia is carrying flowers. She loves flowers.*

**Animal** flōrēs edit. Flōrēs **amat**.
*The animal is eating the flowers. It loves flowers.*

**Regular verbs**—There are four patterns, or groups, of verbs referred to as: the **first conjugation**, the **second conjugation**, the **third conjugation**, and the **fourth conjugation**, hereafter indicated by 1st, 2nd, 3rd, and 4th. Once you have learned the personal pronoun endings for a conjugation, you can attach them to any verb belonging to that conjugation.

**Irregular verbs**—There are some common verbs which do not follow the regular pattern, for instance **esse** *(to be)*. You must learn this verb thoroughly since many verb tenses use the various tenses of **esse** in their formation. Consult your textbook for the conjugation of **esse** and other irregular verbs. You will have to memorize them individually.

To conjugate a verb, you must know the conjugation to which it belongs, its stem, and the personal endings. Let us see how it works:

## How to Conjugate a Verb

Whatever verb you have to conjugate, these are the steps you should follow:

1. CONJUGATION—Establish the conjugation of the verb; i.e., the pattern. The vowel that precedes the -re of the infinitive form (see **What is an Infinitive?**, p. 50) will tell you to which of the four Latin conjugations the verb belongs.

| Conjugation | Ending | Infinitive |        |
| ----------- | ------ | ---------- | ------ |
| 1st         | -āre   | amāre      | *to love* |
| 2nd         | -ēre   | docēre     | *to teach* |
| 3rd         | -ere   | mittere    | *to send* |
| 4th         | -īre   | audīre     | *to hear* |

It is especially important to distinguish between the long and short -e- in the infinitive of verbs for it indicates the difference between the 2nd conjugation (**docēre**) and the 3rd (**mittere**).

Your Latin textbook will also refer to a category of 3rd conjugation verbs called 3rd **-iō**, so called because a characteristic **-i-** appears in several forms: **faciō** *(I do, I make)*, **faciēbam** *(I did, I made)*, **faciam** *(I shall make)*. The infinitive, however, ends in **-ere**, the regular 3rd conjugation infinitive ending.

2. STEM—Find the stem. The infinitive also provides you with a stem called the **present stem** on which the present, imperfect and future tenses are formed. To find this stem, drop the infinitive ending **-re** from the infinitive form.

Here is a sample present stem for a verb of each of the four conjugations:

| Conjugation | Infinitive | Stem   |
| ----------- | ---------- | ------ |
| 1st         | **amāre**  | amā-   |
| 2nd         | **docēre** | docē-  |
| 3rd         | **mittere**| mitte- |
| 4th         | **audīre** | audī-  |

Consult your textbook for irregularities and for the stems to be used for other tenses.

3. PERSONAL ENDINGS—Add the personal endings. The following personal endings are the same for the present, imperfect, and future tenses in the active voice (see p. 84), for all four conjugations. In the imperfect and future tenses the personal endings are added to the stem followed by a tense sign (see pp. 60, 65).

| Person | | Singular | Plural | |
| ------ | --- | -------- | ------ | ---- |
| 1st | I | -ō or -m[1] | we | -mus |
| 2nd | you | -s | you | -tis |
| 3rd | he/she/it | -t | they | -nt |

Let us look at some verbs of the first conjugation so that you can see how the pattern applies to all verbs in the same conjugation.

[1]Your textbook will tell you which tenses use -ō and which use -m as the ending of the first person singular.

- all have an infinitive ending in -āre

    | | |
    |---|---|
    | amāre | *to love* |
    | portāre | *to carry* |
    | cantāre | *to sing* |

- all form their stem by dropping the -re of the infinitive

    amā-          portā-     cantā-

- all add the same personal endings to form the present tense

| Person | | Singular | |
|---|---|---|---|
| 1st | amō[1] | portō[1] | cantō[1] |
| 2nd | amās | portās | cantās |
| 3rd | amat | portat | cantat |
| | | **Plural** | |
| 1st | amāmus | portāmus | cantāmus |
| 2nd | amātis | portātis | cantātis |
| 3rd | amant | portant | cantant |

Your Latin textbook lists the complete pattern for the other three conjugations, some of which have irregularities.

▼▼▼▼▼▼▼▼▼▼▼▼▼▼▼REVIEW ▼▼▼▼▼▼▼▼▼▼▼▼▼▼▼▼

I. Circle the infinitive ending for each Latin verb below.

- On the line provided, indicate the conjugation to which each verb belongs.

1. **cantāre** *(to sing)* _____
2. **vīvere** *(to live)* _____
3. **dēbēre** *(to owe)* _____
4. **mūnīre** *(to fortify)* _____
5. **crēdere** *(to believe)* _____

II. The Latin equivalent of the verb *to praise* is **laudāre.**

- Indicate the stem.
- Write out the Latin present tense conjugation of the verb.

STEM: _____

1ST PER. SING. _____

2ND PER. SING. _____

3RD PER. SING. _____

1ST PER. PL. _____

2ND PER.PL. _____

3RD PER. PL. _____

[1]The first person singular (first principal part) in the first conjugation contracts a + ō to ō, not amaō, but amō.

# 16. WHAT IS MEANT BY TENSE?

The **tense** of a verb indicates when the action of the verb takes place: at the present time, in the past, or in the future. The word for tense comes from the Latin **tempus,** meaning time.

| | |
|---|---|
| **present** | I eat |
| **past** | I ate |
| **future** | I shall eat |

As you can see in the above examples, just by putting the verb in a different tense and without giving any additional information (such as "I eat *now*," or I ate *yesterday*," or "I shall eat *tomorrow*"), you can indicate when the action of the verb takes place.

**IN ENGLISH**
There are six main tenses in English:

| **present** | I eat | **present perfect** | I have eaten |
|---|---|---|---|
| **past** | I ate | **past perfect** | I had eaten |
| **future** | I shall eat | **future perfect** | I shall have eaten |

The listing of the forms of a verb in all six tenses is called a **synopsis.** Above is a synopsis of "eat" in the first person singular.

**IN LATIN**
The six tenses in Latin are divided into sections, a present and a perfect system:

| **Present System** | **Perfect System** |
|---|---|
| present | perfect |
| imperfect | past perfect or pluperfect |
| future | future perfect |

These tenses are discussed in separate sections: **What is the Present Tense?**, p. 58, **What is the Past Tense?**, p. 60, **What is the Past Perfect Tense?**, p. 63, and **What is the Future Tense?**, p. 65, **What is the Future Perfect Tense?**, p. 67.

▼▼▼▼▼▼▼▼▼▼▼▼▼▼▼REVIEW ▼▼▼▼▼▼▼▼▼▼▼▼▼▼▼▼▼

Write a synopsis in the first person singular ("I") for the English verb *think:*

PRESENT _____    PRESENT PERFECT _____

PAST _____    PAST PERFECT _____

FUTURE _____    FUTURE PERFECT _____

## 17. WHAT IS THE PRESENT TENSE?

The **present tense** indicates that the action is going on at the present time. It can be:

- when the speaker is speaking     I *see* you.
- an habitual action                He *smokes* when he is nervous.
- a general truth                   The sun *shines* every day.

**IN ENGLISH**

There are three forms of the verb which, although they have a slightly different meaning, all indicate the present tense.

| | |
|---|---|
| **simple present** | Pan *watches* the beautiful nymph. |
| **present progressive** | Pan *is watching* the beautiful nymph. |
| **present emphatic** | Pan *does watch* the beautiful nymph. |

To ask questions, you need to use the progressive or emphatic form.

*Is* Pan *watching* the beautiful nymph?
*Does* Pan usually *watch* the beautiful nymph?

**IN LATIN**

Only one verb form is needed to indicate the present tense. It is indicated by the ending of the verb added to the stem, without any helping verb such as *is* or *does*. It is very important, therefore, not to translate these English helping verbs; simply put the verb in the present tense.

Pan *watches* the beautiful nymph.
spectat

Pan *is watching* the beautiful nymph.
spectat

Pan *does watch* the beautiful nymph.
spectat

When you are translating a Latin verb in the present tense into English, you will have to choose the most appropriate of the three meanings according to the context.

▼▼▼▼▼▼▼▼▼▼▼▼▼▼▼REVIEW ▼▼▼▼▼▼▼▼▼▼▼▼▼▼▼▼▼▼

Below are two Latin sentences followed by their English translation.

▪ Write the English translation for each verb in the progressive form.
▪ Write the English translation for each verb in the emphatic form.

1.    Puellae aquam sacram **portant.**

*The girls **carry** the sacred water.*

PROGRESSIVE FORM:    The girls _____ the sacred water.

EMPHATIC FORM:    The girls _____ the sacred water.

2.    Virgo Vestal ignem sacram **cūrat.**

The Vestal Virgin *takes care of the sacred fire.*

PROGRESSIVE FORM:    The Vestal Virgin _____ the sacred fire.

EMPHATIC FORM:    The Vestal Virgin _____ the sacred fire.

## 18. WHAT IS THE PAST TENSE?

The **past tense** is used to express an action that occurred previously, some time before the present time.

**IN ENGLISH**
There are several verb forms that indicate that the action took place in the past.

| | |
|---|---|
| **simple past** | I worked |
| **past progressive** | I was working |
| **past emphatic** | I did work |
| **present perfect** | I have worked |

The simple past is called "simple" because it is a **simple tense**; i.e., it consists of one word *(worked* in the example above). The other past tenses are called **verb phrases** or **compound tenses**; i.e., they consist of more than one word, an auxiliary plus a main verb *(was working, did work).*

**IN LATIN**
There are two Latin tenses which correspond to the four verbal forms listed above: the **imperfect** and the **perfect** (called the present perfect in English).

### The Imperfect Tense

The imperfect is formed with the present stem + the imperfect tense sign -**bā**- + the personal endings. The conjugation is regular, except that the 1st person singular ends in -**m: spectā-** + -**ba-** + -**m** → **spectābam** *(I watched).*

There are several other English verb forms that indicate that the imperfect should be used in Latin:

1. When the English verb form is in the past progressive tense, as in *was singing, were working.*

>    *The nymphs **were watching** the stag in the woods.*
>    Nymphae cervum in silvīs **spectābant.**
>                                      imperfect

2. When the English verb form is in the past emphatic tense.

> *The women **did work** in the fields.*
> Fēminae in agrīs **labōrābant.**
> |
> imperfect

> ***Did** the women **work** in the fields?*
> **Labōrābantne** fēminae in agrīs?
> |
> **-ne** added to first word changes sentence to question

3. When the English verb form includes, or could include, the helping verb *used to.*

> *Narcissus **used to watch** his reflection in a pool.*
> Narcissus in stagnō imāginem suam **spectābat.**
> |
> imperfect

## The Perfect Tense

The perfect tense is based on the third principal part of the verb (see **What are the Principal Parts of a Verb?**, p. 47) which provides the **perfect stem**. This stem is not only used in the perfect tense, but to form many other verb forms.

> principal parts →    amō, amāre, **amāvī,** amātum
> |
> perfect

To find the perfect stem drop the final -**ī** of the third principal part.

> perfect stem →    amāv-

The perfect tense of all four conjugations is formed with the perfect stem + the perfect personal endings.

| Person | Singular | | Plural | |
|---|---|---|---|---|
| 1st | I | -ī | we | -imus |
| 2nd | you | -istī | you | -istis |
| 3rd | he/she/it | -it | they | -ērunt |

The perfect tense, **amāv** + -**ī** (**amāvī**) can be translated as *I loved, I have loved,* and *I did love.*

## Selection of the Perfect or the Imperfect

As a general guideline, remember the following:

**imperfect** → tells "what was going on" or "how things used to be"
**perfect** → tells "what happened"

Since the perfect and the imperfect indicate actions that took place during the same time period in the past, you will often find the two tenses appearing in the same sentence or a story.

> *Callisto **was walking** through the woods when suddenly she **saw** a bear.*
>> Both actions "walking" and "saw" are taking place in the past.
>> What was going on? Callisto was walking → imperfect
>> What happened? she saw a bear → perfect

> Callistō per silvās **ambulābat** cum subitō ursam **vīdit.**
>> imperfect                                            perfect

Your Latin textbook will give you additional guidelines to help you choose the appropriate tense. You should practice analyzing English paragraphs. Pick out the verbs in the past and indicate for each one if you would put it in the perfect or in the imperfect. Sometimes both tenses are possible, but usually one of the two is more logical.

▼▼▼▼▼▼▼▼▼▼▼▼▼▼▼REVIEW ▼▼▼▼▼▼▼▼▼▼▼▼▼▼▼▼

The verbs in the following paragraph are in *italics*.
- Circle the verbs that would be put in the imperfect in Latin.
- Underline the verbs that would be put in the perfect in Latin.

I *was sitting* at home in the evening watching television. The dog *was sleeping* beside me, and I *was* not afraid because he *was* a good watch dog. My husband *was working* late, and my son *was sleeping* upstairs. Suddenly I *heard* a noise in the kitchen. The dog *sat up* and *barked*. I *ran* upstairs and *called* the police on the phone. They *arrived* in minutes and *found* that a broom had fallen out of the closet.

## 19. WHAT IS THE PAST PERFECT TENSE?

The **past perfect** tense (also called the **pluperfect** in Latin) is used to express an action completed in the past before some other specific action or event occurred in the past.

**IN ENGLISH**
The past perfect is a verb phrase formed with the auxiliary *had* + the past participle of the main verb: *had eaten, had taken.* The past perfect is used when two actions happened at different times in the past, and you want to make it clear which of the actions preceded the other.

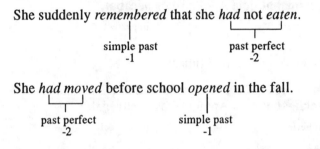

In both sentences, actions -1 and -2 occurred in the past, but action -2 preceded -1. Therefore, action -2 is in the past perfect.

**IN LATIN**
Another name for the Latin past perfect tense is **pluperfect.** It is formed with the perfect stem + the imperfect forms of **esse** to form a single word: **cantāv- + -eram → cantāveram** *(I had sung),* **cantāverās** *(you had sung),* etc.

As in English, a verb is put in the pluperfect tense in order to stress that the action of that verb took place before the action of a verb in either the perfect or the imperfect.

In Latin and English the same relationship exists between the tense of the verb and the time when the action takes place.

Observe the sequence of events expressed by the past tenses in the following time-line:

**VERB TENSE:**   Pluperfect       Perfect or          Present
                              Imperfect
                **-2**               **-1**               **0**

—————————x————————————x————————————————x

**TIME ACTION TAKES PLACE:**     $0 \rightarrow$ now
                                   $-1 \rightarrow$ before 0
                                   $-2 \rightarrow$ before -1

Same verb tense = same moment in time:

> *Niobe was weeping because Apollo was killing her sons.*
> Niobē **lacrimābat** quia Apollo fīliōs **necābat.**
>      imperfect                     imperfect
>        -1                           -1

Different verb tenses = different times:

> *Niobe was weeping because Apollo had killed her sons.*
> Niobē **lacrimābat** quia Apollo fīliōs **necāverat.**
>      imperfect                     pluperfect
>        -1                           -2

▼▼▼▼▼▼▼▼▼▼▼▼▼▼▼▼REVIEW ▼▼▼▼▼▼▼▼▼▼▼▼▼▼▼▼

The verbs of the sentences below are in **boldface**. In the parentheses, indicate the tense of the verbs : "-1" for the past tense and "-2" for the past perfect.

1. Often the gods **came** to earth to see what the people **had done.**

                     (  )                             (  )

2. In one village the people **were** cruel, and they **had stoned** strangers.

                           (  )              (  )

3. Only Baucis and Philemon **were** kind, because they **had welcomed** the strangers.          (  )                      (  )

## 20. WHAT IS THE FUTURE TENSE?

The **future tense** is used to describe an action which will take place in time to come, the future.

**IN ENGLISH**
The future is expressed by a verb phrase consisting of the auxiliary verb *will* or *shall* + the dictionary form of the main verb.

> Thisbe *will arrive* first.
> Pyramus *will grieve* for her death.
> We *shall listen* to the story.[1]

In conversation, *shall* and *will* are often shortened to '*ll:* You'*ll do* it tomorrow; *I'll listen* to the music. In practice most people express future time by using the verb phrase "is going to..." or the present tense.

> Pyramus *is going to* be late.
> Pyramus will grieve when he *sees* Thisbe's bloody veil.

**IN LATIN**
You do not need an auxiliary verb to show that the action will take place in the future. Instead, Latin uses a **tense sign**; i.e, one or two letters inserted between the stem and the personal endings. The future tense is formed with the present stem + the tense sign for the future: **-bi-** (for 1st and 2nd conjugations) or **-ē-** (for 3rd and 4th conjugations) + the personal endings: **cantābit** *(he/she/it will sing)*, **docēbimus** *(we shall teach)*, **mittēs** *(you will send)*, **audient** *(they will hear)*.

The use of the future in Latin corresponds to the use of the future in English.

> Thisbē prīma **adveniet.**
>      | 
>     future
> *Thisbe **will arrive** first.*

> Pȳramus mortem eius **dolēbit.**
>       | 
>      future
> *Pyramus **will grieve** for her death.*

---

[1]These sentences are based on the sad tale of Pyramus and Thisbe, young lovers whose marriage is prevented by their parents. They agree to meet secretly and through mistakes kill themselves thinking each has caused the other's death.

## Nota Bene

While English occasionally uses the present tense after expressions such as *as soon as*, *when*, and *by the time*, which introduce an action that will take place in the future, Latin uses the future tense (the numbers 2 and 0 for the tenses refer to the time-line on p. 67).

*Pyramus will grieve when he sees Thisbe's scarf.*

future  
2

present (future time)  
0

Pyramus **dolēbit** cum velāmina Thisbēs **vidēbit.**

future  
2

future  
2

Latin is much stricter than English in its use of tenses.

▼▼▼▼▼▼▼▼▼▼▼▼▼▼▼▼REVIEW ▼▼▼▼▼▼▼▼▼▼▼▼▼▼▼▼▼

The verbs of the sentences below are in **boldface**. Circle the tense of the verb in the English sentence and what the tense would be in Latin: P (present) or F (future).

1. If Pyramus and Thisbe **fall** in love, they **will want** to meet secretly.

ENGLISH:          P  F          P  F

LATIN:             P  F          P  F

2. When Thisbe **sees** the lion, she **will hide** in a cave.

ENGLISH:     P  F          P  F

LATIN:       P  F          P  F

3. When Pyramus **sees** Thisbe's bloody veil, he'**ll kill** himself.

ENGLISH:       P  F               P  F

LATIN:         P  F               P  F

## 21. WHAT IS THE FUTURE PERFECT TENSE?

The **future perfect** tense is used to express an action which will have happened before another action in the future or before a specific time in the future.

**IN ENGLISH**
The future perfect is formed with the auxiliary *will have* (or *shall have*) + the past participle of the main verb: *I will have walked, she will (shall) have gone*, etc. In conversation *will* is shortened to *'ll* or, in some cases, dropped altogether and *have* or *has* is shortened to *"'ve"* or *"'s."*

> I'll see you as soon as I *will have finished*. [rarely used]
> I'll see you as soon as I *'ll have finished*.
> I'll see you as soon as I *have finished*.
> I'll see you as soon as I *'ve finished*.

> He *will have left* before the teacher *gives* the exam tomorrow.
> future perfect      present (future time implied)
> 1      2

> Actions 1 and 2 will occur in the future, but action 1 will be completed before 2. Therefore, action 1 is in the future perfect.

**IN LATIN**
The future perfect is formed with the perfect stem + the future forms of esse to form a single word: **cantāv + -erō → cantāverō** (*I will have sung*).

As in English, a verb is put in the future perfect tense in order to stress that the action of the verb will take place before the action of a verb in the future, or before a specific future time.

Observe the sequence of events expressed by the future tenses in the following time-line:

| VERB TENSE: | Present | Future perfect | Future |
|---|---|---|---|
| | **0** | **1** | **2** |

TIME ACTION TAKES PLACES:   $0 \rightarrow$ now
$1 \rightarrow$ after 0 and before 2
$2 \rightarrow$ after 0 and after 1

In the following examples, notice that actions taking place at point "1" are in the future perfect tense in both languages. (Remember that English often uses the present tense when the future is implied, see p. 66.)

> When Pyramus *arrives, Thisbe will have left.*
>
> present (future time implied)    future perfect
>            2                              1

> Cum Pyramus **adveniet,** Thisbē **discesserit.**
>             future                 future perfect

Latin also uses the future perfect to express future conditions (see p. 114 in **What are Conditional Sentences?**).

▼▼▼▼▼▼▼▼▼▼▼▼▼▼▼▼REVIEW ▼▼▼▼▼▼▼▼▼▼▼▼▼▼▼▼▼▼

The verbs of the sentences below are in **boldface.** Circle the tense of the verb in the English sentence and what the tense would be in Latin: P (present tense), F (future tense), or FP (future perfect).

1. Thisbe **will kill** herself when she **sees** Pyramus dying.

ENGLISH:   P   F   FP            P   F   FP

LATIN:     P   F   FP            P   F   FP

2. The blood of Pyramus **will have changed** the color of the fruit of the mulberry tree by the time Thisbe **returns.**

ENGLISH:          P   F   FP            P   F   FP

LATIN:            P   F   FP            P   F   FP

3. When Thisbe **returns,** Pyramus already **will have killed** himself.

ENGLISH:       P   F   FP              P   F   FP

LATIN:         P   F   FP              P   F   FP

## 22. WHAT IS AN AUXILIARY VERB?

A verb is called an **auxiliary verb** or **helping verb** when it helps another verb form one of its tenses (see **What is Meant by Tense?**, p. 57). When it is used alone, it functions as a main verb.

Jupiter *is watching* the nymph.        Jupiter *is* a god.
    auxiliary  main verb             main verb
    verb
    └─verb phrase─┘

Latona *has called* her children.        Latona *has* two children.
    auxiliary  main verb             main verb
    verb
    └─verb phrase─┘

The soldiers *did cross* the river.        The soldiers *did* their exercises.
    auxiliary  main verb             main verb
    verb
    └─verb phrase─┘

An auxiliary verb plus a main verb form a **compound tense**, also called a **verb phrase**.

**IN ENGLISH**
There are several auxiliary verbs: forms of *to have, to be,* and *to do*, as well as a series of auxiliary words such as *will, would, may, might, must, can, could* which are used to change the meaning of the main verb.

Auxiliary verbs and words serve many purposes:

▪ to indicate the tense of the main verb (present, past, future — see **What is Meant by Tense?**, p. 57) in a verb phrase:

    **present**           Jupiter *is watching* the nymph.
                          auxiliary *to be*
                            └─verb phrase ─┘

    **present perfect**    Latona *has seen* her children die.
                        auxiliary *to have*
                           └─verb phrase ─┘

> **future**                    Apollo *will chase* Daphne.
>                               auxiliary *will*
>                               └─verb phrase─┘

- to help form the perfect tenses (see **What is the Past Tense?**, p. 60; **What is the Past Perfect [Pluperfect] Tense?**, p. 63; and **What is the Future Perfect Tense?**, p. 65)

> Latona *has called* her children.
>        └──┬──┘
>       present perfect

> Pan *had breathed* over the reeds.
>     └──┬──┘
>    past perfect

- to indicate the passive voice (see **What is Meant by Active and Passive Voice?**, p. 84)

> The story *is read* by many students.
>           └─┬─┘
>        present passive

> The play *was performed* by experienced actors.
>          └───┬───┘
>         past passive

- to help form the progressive forms of the present and past tenses (see **What is the Present Tense?**, p. 58 and **What is the Past Tense?**, p. 60)

> Jupiter *is watching* the nymph.
>         └──┬──┘
>       present progressive

> Apollo *was chasing* Daphne.
>        └──┬──┘
>      past progressive

- to help form questions and to make sentences negative (see **What are Declarative and Interrogative Sentences?**, p. 105)

> *Does* Mary *read* a book?
> Mary *does not read* a book.

- to help form the emphatic forms of the present and past tenses (see **What is the Present Tense?**, p. 58 and **What is the Past Tense?**, p. 60)

  Jupiter *does like* to watch the nymphs.

  present emphatic

  Pan *did make* a flute out of reeds.

  past emphatic

- to help form ideas of possibility or probability (see **What is the Subjunctive Mood?**, p. 92)

  The Argonauts *may come* tomorrow.

### IN LATIN

Tenses or ideas that are composed of a verb phrase in English are usually expressed by a single verb in Latin.

  Jupiter *is watching* the nymph.

  In English: present progressive
  In Latin: present → **spectat**

  Latona *has called* her children.

  In English: present perfect
  In Latin: present perfect → **vocāvit**

  The story *is read* by many students.

  In English: present passive
  In Latin: present passive → **legitur**

  Jupiter *does love* the nymphs.

  In English: present emphatic
  In Latin: present → **amat**

*Did* the soldiers *cross* the river?

In English: to formulate a question (past)
In Latin: perfect + ne[1] → **Trānsiēruntne**

Apollo *will kill* the sons of Niobe.

In English: to formulate future
In Latin: future → **necābit**

The Argonauts *may come* tomorrow.

In English: *may* to indicate possibility
In Latin: present subjunctive → **reveniant**

▼▼▼▼▼▼▼▼▼▼▼▼▼▼▼REVIEW ▼▼▼▼▼▼▼▼▼▼▼▼▼▼▼▼
Underline the verbs and verb phrases in the following paragraph.

Because Phaethon was always asking questions about his father, his mother sent him to the sun god Apollo, his father. Phaethon asked proof about his parentage, and he demanded permission to drive the chariot of the sun across the sky for a day. Apollo was feeling sad because his son had requested such a gift as proof. When Phaethon insisted, his father sorrowfully yoked the wild horses of the sun chariot. The horses could feel the weak hands on the reins, and they plunged wildly through the sky alternately burning and freezing the earth. Finally Jupiter hurled a thunderbolt to save the earth, but Phaethon died in a tragic fall from the chariot.

---

[1] To make a sentence into a question, Latin adds **-ne** to the first word, usually the verb.

# 23. WHAT IS A PARTICIPLE?

A **participle** is a verb form which is part verb and part adjective; it is called a **verbal adjective**.

In English, there are two participles: the present participle and the past participle. In Latin, there are three participles: the present, the past, and the future participles.

## The Present Participle

**IN ENGLISH**
The present participle is easy to recognize because it is the *-ing* form of the verb: *running, working, studying.*

The present participle has three functions:

1. as part of a verb phrase to form the progressive forms (see p. 58)

Theseus *is entering* the labryinth.[1]
    └──┬──┘
    verb phrase

Ariadne *was trying* to help Theseus.
    └──┬──┘
    verb phrase

2. as an adjective to describe a noun or pronoun (see pp. 74, 116)

Theseus was an *inspiring* hero.
attributive adjective describing the noun *hero*

He was *inspiring*.
predicate adjective describing the pronoun *he*

3. as an adjective introducing a participial phrase (see p. 74)

Theseus, *seeing* the Minotaur, was not afraid.
The entire phrase *seeing the Minotaur* works as an adjective modifying Theseus.

No one saw Theseus *killing* the Minotaur.
The entire phrase *killing the Minotaur* works as an adjective modifying Theseus.

---

[1]Theseus, aided by the princess Ariadne who gave him a ball of string, entered the maze called the labyrinth and killed the Minotaur, a creature half-man and half-bull.

**IN LATIN**

The present participle is called the **present active participle**, since it is always active in meaning (see **What is Meant by Active and Passive Voice?**, p. 84). It is formed with the present stem of the verb + **-ns** (nom. sing.), **-ntis** (gen. sing.). It is an adjective of the third declension (Group B, see p. 120), declined in all cases, singular and plural: **cantāns, cantantis** *(singing)*, **docēns, docentis** *(teaching)*, **mittēns, mittentis** *(sending)*, **capiēns, capientis** *(taking)*, **audiēns, audientis** *(hearing)*. Since it is an adjective, it must agree in case, gender, and number with the noun or pronoun it modifies.

The present active participle has two functions:

1. as a descriptive adjective

> *Theseus was an inspiring hero.*
> 1. Noun modified: hero
> 2. Case: *Hero* is predicate word → nominative
> 3. Gender and number: **Hērōs** is masculine singular.
> Thēseus erat hēros **inspirāns**.
>                    |
>                    present active participle
>                    nominative masculine singular

> *Theseus saw the burning palace.*
> 1. Noun modified: palace
> 2. Case: *Palace* is direct object → accusative
> 3. Gender and number: **Rēgia** *(palace)* is feminine singular.
> Thēseus rēgiam **conflagrantem** vīdit.
>                       |
>                       present active participle
>                       accusative feminine singular

2. as an adjective introducing a participial phrase

> *Theseus, seeing the Minotaur, was not afraid.*
> 1. Noun modified: Theseus
> 2. Case: *Theseus* is the subject → nominative
> 3. Gender and number: **Thēseus** is masculine singular.
> Thēseus Mīnōtaurum **vidēns** nōn timēbat.
>                          |
>                          present active participle
>                          nominative masculine singular

> *No one saw Theseus killing the Minotaur.*
> 1. Noun modified: Theseus
> 2. Case: *Theseus* is direct object → accusative
> 3. Gender and number: **Thēseus** is masculine singular.
> Nēmo Thēseum Mīnōtaurum **necantem** vīdit.
>                              |
>                              present active participle
>                              accusative masculine singular

## *Nota Bene*

1. Remember that the English tenses formed with an auxiliary verb *to be* + present participle *(she is studying, they were dancing)* correspond to a simple Latin tense. Consult the sections on tenses of verbs.

> *Orpheus is singing.*[1]
> └──┬──┘
>    present progressive

> Orpheus **cantat.**
>          |
>        present

> *The animals were listening.*
>            └────┬────┘
>               past progressive

> Animālia **audiēbant.**
>             |
>          imperfect

> *Eurydice will be coming soon.*
>          └────┬────┘
>           future progressive

> Eurydicē **veniet.**
>            |
>         future

2. What might appear to be a present participle (a verbal adjective) because it is a verb form ending in *-ing* could also be a gerund (a verbal noun). Be sure to consult the section **What is a Verbal Noun (a Gerund)?**, p. 81, in which there is a chart summarizing the various English *-ing* forms and their Latin equivalents on p. 83.

### The Past Participle

**IN ENGLISH**

The past participle is the verb form used following *"I have"*: *I have taken, I have helped, I have written.* The "regular" verbs form their past participle with the dictionary form of the verb + *-ed, -d,* or *-t.*

---

[1] The wedding of the famous singer Orpheus was spoiled when the bride, Eurydice, was bitten by a snake and died. She went to the Underworld, but Orpheus, who could move even animals and rocks with his music, persuaded the king and queen of that region to allow Eurydice to return to Earth. He was not allowed to look back at her, but unfortunately he could not resist a backward glance. She disappeared a second time, this time forever.

| Dictionary form | Past participle |
|---|---|
| help | helped |
| hear | heard |
| walk | walked |
| burn | burned or burnt |

The irregular verbs form their past participle in no set manner, and each must be learned separately.

| Dictionary form | Past participle |
|---|---|
| eat | eaten |
| teach | taught |
| write | written |
| sing | sung |

The past participle has three functions:

1. as part of a verb phrase

- in an active sentence (see **What is Meant by Active and Passive Voice?**, p. 84)

   The mighty city of Troy *has fallen*.[1]
   Many Trojan heroes *have died*.

- in a passive sentence

   Many Trojan heroes *were killed* in the war.
   The Trojan horse *was dragged* into the city.

2. as an attributive descriptive adjective to describe a noun or pronoun

   The *captured city* was burned by the Greeks.
   describes the noun *city*

   Hecuba buried her *murdered sons*.
   describes the noun *sons*

3. to introduce a participial phrase

   Troy, *captured by the Greeks*, was burned.
   The Trojan women, *dragged by the hair*, were carried off.

**IN LATIN**

The past participle is called the **perfect passive participle**, since it is normally passive in meaning. The perfect passive participle must be

---

[1]The Trojan War was fought by the Greeks to recover the beautiful Queen Helen, who had been abducted by the Trojan Paris, son of Priam, king of Troy. The Greeks finally destroyed the city of Troy, having entered it through the ruse of a Wooden Horse. They murdered Priam, his sons, and most of the Trojans, but took the Queen Hecuba as a captive. Helen was returned to her husband.

learned with each verb as the fourth principal part (see **What are the Principal Parts of a Verb?**, p. 47) ending in **-tum** or **-sum**. It is an adjective of the first and second declension (Group A, see p. 119): **cantātum** *(having been sung)*, **doctum** *(having been taught)*, **missum** *(having been sent)*, **audītum** *(having been heard)*. Since it is an adjective, it must agree in case, gender, and number with the noun or pronoun it modifies.

The perfect passive participle has three major functions:

1. as a part of a verb phrase to form perfect tenses of the passive voice

> *The city of Troy was **burned** by the Greeks.*
>> 1. Noun modified: city
>> 2. Case: *City* is subject → nominative
>> 3. Gender and number: **Urbs** *(city)* is feminine singular.
>
> Urbs Trōia ā Graecīs **incensa** est.
>
> perfect passive participle (nom. fem. sing.) + **est**

2. as a descriptive attributive adjective

> *The Greeks burned the **captured** city.*
>> 1. Noun modified: city
>> 2. Case: *City* is direct object → accusative
>> 3. Gender and number: **Urbem** *(city)* is feminine singular.
>
> Graecī urbem **captam** incendērunt.
>
> perfect passive participle (acc. fem. sing.)

> *Hecuba buried her **murdered** sons.*
>> 1. Noun modified: sons
>> 2. Case: *Sons* is direct object → accusative
>> 3. Gender and number: **Fīliōs** *(sons)* is masculine plural.
>
> Hecuba fīliōs **necātōs** sepelīvit.
>
> perfect passive participle (acc. masc. pl.)

3. as an adjective in a participial phrase

   ▪ introducing the participial phrase

> participial phrase
>
> *Driven by wind, the Greek ships came to Troy.*
>> 1. Noun modified: ships
>> 2. Case: *Ships* is subject → nominative
>> 3. Gender and number: **Nāvēs** *(ships)* is feminine plural.
>
> **Pulsae** ventō nāvēs Graecae Trōiam advēnērunt.
>
> perfect passive participle (nom. fem. pl.)

participial phrase

*The Trojans saw the horse **left behind** by the Greeks.*
1. Noun modified: horse
2. Case: *Horse* is direct object → accusative
3. Gender and number: **Equum** *(horse)* is masculine singular.

Troiāni equum ā Graecīs **relictum** vīdērunt.

perfect passive participle (acc. masc. sing.)

▪ within an ablative absolute

The **ablative absolute** construction is very common in Latin: it consists of two words in the ablative case, most often a noun and a participle. Although grammatically independent (and therefore
"absolute") of the subject or the object of the main clause (see
pp. 100-2), it is logically connected to explain the circumstances
surrounding the action of the main verb.

ablative absolute

Mīnōtaurō **necāto**, Theseus ab īnsulā discessit.

perfect passive participle
modifying **Mīnōtaurō**
both in ablative masculine singular

*The Minotaur **having been killed**, Theseus left the island.*
*After the Minotaur had been killed, Theseus left the island.*

## Nota Bene
Keep in mind that the equivalent of English active tenses formed with
the auxiliary verb *have* + past participle *(have seen)* do not use participles in Latin. The English verb phrase corresponds to a Latin tense:

*I **have seen** the beautiful city of Troy.*

verb phrase

Urbem Trōiam pulchram **vīdī**.

perfect tense

## The Future Participles

**IN ENGLISH**

There are no future participle verb forms. There are, however, English constructions that require the use of future participles in Latin.

**IN LATIN**

There are two future participles, active and passive (see p. 84). They are verbal adjectives, verb forms used as adjectives. Let us consider them separately since each has different uses.

The **future active participle** is used to express the idea that someone is about to perform an action and corresponds to the English expression "about to" + the present form of the verb (I am *about to leave.*) It is formed with the stem of the perfect passive participle (4th principal part of the verb) + **-ūrus, -ūra, -ūrum**. It is an adjective of the first and second declension (Group A, p. 119): **ventūrus, -a, -um**, *(about to come)*, **futūrus, -a, -um** *(about to be)*. Since it is an adjective, it must agree in case, gender, and number with the noun it modifies.

> *The gladiators **about to die** saluted the emperor.*
> Gladiātōrēs **moritūrī** imperātōrem salutāvērunt.
>         |
>         future active participle
>         nom. masc. pl. modifying **gladiātōrēs**

The future active participle is often used with a form of **esse** to express an imminent action, an action about to take place. This usage is called the **active periphrastic**, from the word periphrasis meaning speaking in a round-about manner. It is a round-about way of expressing future time.

> *The Sirens **are about to sing**.*
> Sirēnēs **cantātūrae sunt**.[1]
>       |
>       active periphrastic
>       future active participle + **sunt**

The **future passive participle** is commonly called the **gerundive**. It is formed from the present stem + **-ndus, -nda, -ndum**. It is an adjective of the first and second declension (Group A, p. 119): **cantandus, -a, -um** *(about to be sung)*; **legendus, -a, -um** *(about to be read)*. Since it is an adjective, it must agree with the noun it modifies in case, gender, and number.

---

[1]Compare to the regular future **cantābunt**, *will sing.*

Librum **legendum** habeō.

future passive participle (gerundive)
acc. masc. sing. modifying **librum**

*I have a book to be read.*
*I have a book which should be read.*

Although it literally means "about to be" + the past participle, it is not so much the fact that the act will take place in the future that is being expressed, but rather the idea of obligation or necessity to perform the act.

The future passive participle (the gerundive) is often used with a form of **esse** as a verb phrase expressing obligation or necessity. This usage is called the **passive periphrastic**.

Hic liber tibi **legendus est**.

passive periphrastic
fut. pass. part. (gerundive) + **est**
nom. sing. masc. modifying **liber**

*This book must be read by you.*

With a passive periphrastic, the "by you" idea (**tibi**) is expressed by the dative case .

▼▼▼▼▼▼▼▼▼▼▼▼▼▼▼REVIEW ▼▼▼▼▼▼▼▼▼▼▼▼▼▼▼▼

Underline the participles in the sentences below.

▪ Circle whether each participle is used as an adjective (A) or as part of a verb phrase (VP).

1. Theseus, growing up, did not know that his father was king of Athens.     A   VP

2. Theseus found the sword and sandals which had been left by his father.     A   VP

3. Desiring to meet his father, Theseus set out for Athens.     A   VP

4. Youths and maidens were chosen by lot to go to Crete.     A   VP

5. Theseus volunteered to go with the chosen youths.     A   VP

# 24. WHAT IS A VERBAL NOUN (A GERUND)?

A **gerund** is a verb form which is part verb and part noun; it is called a **verbal noun.**

### IN ENGLISH
The verbal noun, the gerund, is formed with the dictionary form of the verb + *-ing*: *talking, walking*. It can function in a sentence in almost any way that a noun can: as a subject, object of a verb or of a preposition.

> *Singing* is an art.
> noun from the verb *to sing*
> subject of the sentence

> Do you enjoy *singing?*
> noun from the verb *to sing*
> direct object of verb *to enjoy*

> The art of *singing* is difficult.
> noun from the verb *to sing*
> object of the preposition *of*

Since the English *-ing* form of the verb can be part of a verb phrase, a verbal adjective (present participle), or a verbal noun (gerund), it is important to distinguish among these three uses in order to choose the correct Latin equivalent.

> Maria is *singing*.
> verb phrase
> present tense

> He was a *singing* musician.
> verbal adjective
> present participle

> *Singing* is an art.
> verbal noun
> gerund

See chart on p. 83.

**IN LATIN**

The gerund is a neuter noun of the second declension formed from the present stem of the verb + **-ndī** (gen.), **-ndō** (dat.), **-ndum** (acc.), **-ndō** (abl.). It does not exist in the nominative, since an infinitive is used for the subject in Latin.

Ars **cantandī** difficilis est.

genitive of gerund (no preposition in Latin)

*The art of singing is difficult.*

object of preposition *of*

Amāre discit **amandō**.

ablative of gerund (no preposition in Latin)

*He learns to love by loving.*

object of preposition *by*

As in English, the verbal noun can function in any way that a noun can function, except as the subject or direct object of the sentence. When the verbal noun is the subject of the sentence or the direct object of the verb, Latin uses the infinitive of the verb.

**Cantāre** est ars.

infinitive

*Singing is an art.*

subject

Amāsne **cantāre**?

infinitive

*Do you like singing (to sing)?*

direct object

## Summary

It is important to distinguish between the English *-ing* forms. For reference, here is a chart summarizing the various English *-ing* forms and their Latin equivalents.

| English -ing | | Latin equivalent |
|---|---|---|
| **Verb phrase** | | |
| auxiliary + present | $\longrightarrow$ | various tenses |
| ex.: *is singing* | | present |
| *was singing* | | past |
| *will be singing* | | future |
| **Adjective** | | |
| present participle | $\longrightarrow$ | present active participle |
| ex.: *singing* musician | | present stem + **-ns, -ntis** |
| **Noun (gerund)** | | |
| subject of sentence | $\longrightarrow$ | infinitive |
| ex.: *Singing* is an art. | | |
| direct object of sentence | $\longrightarrow$ | infinitive |
| ex. Do you like *singing*? | | |
| **Other functions** | $\longrightarrow$ | gerund |
| ex.: *of, to,* or *by singing* | | present stem + **-ndī, -ndum, -ndō**[1] |

▼▼▼▼▼▼▼▼▼▼▼▼▼▼▼▼REVIEW ▼▼▼▼▼▼▼▼▼▼▼▼▼▼▼▼▼▼

Circle the *-ing* word in the sentences below.
- Circle whether the *-ing* word in the sentences below is a gerund (G), a participle (P), or part of a verb phrase (VP).

1. Hoping to kill the Minotaur, Theseus went to Crete.   G   P   VP

2. Theseus devoted himself to training for the encounter
   with the Minotaur.   G   P   VP

3. Theseus was always training himself as a wrestler.   G   P   VP

4. The youths had little hope of escaping.   G   P   VP

5. By dancing with the bull, Theseus entertained the Cretans.   G   P   VP

---

[1]Except for 3rd -iō and 4th conjugation, which add an -i to the stem.

## 25. WHAT IS MEANT BY ACTIVE AND PASSIVE VOICE?

The voice of the verb refers to the relationship between the verb and its subject. There are two voices: active and passive.

The **active voice**—A sentence is said to be in the active voice when the verb expresses what the subject of the verb is or does. In this instance, the verb is called an **active verb**.

> The king touches the food.[1]
>   subject   verb   direct object

The subject, *the king*, performs the action of the verb, *touches*, and the direct object, *the food*, is the receiver of the action.

The **passive voice**—A sentence is said to be in the passive voice when the verb expresses what is done to the subject by someone or something. In this instance the verb is called a **passive verb**.

> The food is touched by the king.
>   subject   verb phrase   agent

The subject, *the food*, is not the performer of the action of the verb, *is touched*, but is having the action performed upon it. The doer of the action, *the king*, is called the **agent**.

**IN ENGLISH**

The passive voice is expressed by the verb *to be* conjugated in the proper tense + the past participle of the main verb. Note that the tense of the sentence is indicated by the tense of the auxiliary verb *to be*.

> The food *is touched* by the king.
>   subject   verb phrase   agent
>         present passive

> The race *was won* by the man.
>   subject   verb phrase   agent
>         past passive

> The nymph *will be chased* by the god.
>   subject   verb phrase   agent
>         future passive

---

[1] King Midas asked for and received the golden touch as a favor from a god. The gift seemed a blessing at first when everything turned to gold, but it became a curse when the king tried to eat and drink.

**IN LATIN**

Unlike English verbs, not all passive verbs are expressed with an auxiliary verb. We shall divide passive verbs according to the way they are formed: 1. the present, imperfect, and future tenses and 2. the perfect tenses.

### Present, Imperfect and Future Tenses In the Passive Voice

The present, imperfect, and future passive is expressed by special passive endings, without an auxiliary verb. These endings are added to the present stem, with the appropriate tense signs for the imperfect (see p. 60) and the future (see p. 65).

The same passive endings are used for the present, imperfect, and future tenses:

| Person | Singular | | Plural | |
|--------|----------|------|--------|--------|
| 1st | I | -r | we | -mur |
| 2nd | you | -ris | you | -minī |
| 3rd | he/she/it | -tur | they | -ntur |

PRESENT: present stem + passive endings

Cibus ā rēge **tangitur.**
*The food is touched by the king.*

IMPERFECT: present stem + **-bā-** + passive endings

Cibus ā rēge **tangēbātur.**
*The food was touched by the king.*

FUTURE: present stem + **-bi-** or **-e-** + passive endings

Cibus ā rēge **tangētur.**
*The food will be touched by the king.*

The passive endings are easily distinguished from the active endings.

| **Present passive** | **Present active** |
|---------------------|--------------------|
| Cibus ā rēge **tangitur.** | Rēx cibum **tangit.** |
| *The food is touched by the king.* | *The king touches the food.* |

### Perfect Tenses In the Passive Voice

The perfect, past perfect, and future perfect passive tenses require the use of an auxiliary verb. The perfect passive participle + a form of **esse** conjugated in the appropriate tenses form a verb phrase.

Remember that perfect passive participles are adjectives. Therefore, they must agree with the nouns they modify in case (always nominative subjects), gender, and number.

PERFECT: perfect passive participle + **esse** in present active

Cibus **tactus est**.

nom.
masc. sing   perfect

*The food **has been touched**.*

PAST PERFECT (PLUPERFECT): perfect passive participle + esse in the imperfect active

Cibus **tactus erat**.
*The food **had been touched**.*

FUTURE PERFECT: perfect passive participle + **esse** in the future active

Cibus **tactus erit**.
*The food **will have been touched**.*

## The Agent

In Latin the agent is expressed in one of two ways depending on whether it is a person or a thing:

When the agent is a person, the **ablative of agent** is used: the preposition ā (**ab** before a vowel) + the ablative case.

ā rēge    *by the king*

When the agent is a thing, the **ablative of means** is used: the ablative without a preposition.

ventō    *by the wind*

## Deponent Verbs

There is a type of verb particular to Latin which you must learn to recognize. These verbs have mostly passive forms, i.e. they are conjugated like passive verbs, but they have active meanings. They are called **deponent verbs** from the Latin verb **dēpōnere**, *to lay aside*, because they have *laid aside* their passive meaning. Your Latin textbook will go over the conjugation of these verbs which have only three principal parts: e.g. **loquor, loquī, locutus sum**.

Note the difference in ending between two verbs related to speech: **dīcit** *(he says)*, an active verb in the present tense, and **loquitur** *(he is speaking)*, a deponent verb in the present tense.

> **Dīcit** me esse amicum.
> *He says that I am his friend.*

> **Loquitur** cum amīcō.
> *He speaks with his friend.*

## Nota Bene

English does not have deponent verbs. When you learn these verbs be sure to remember that their meaning is active, although their form is passive.

▼▼▼▼▼▼▼▼▼▼▼▼▼▼REVIEW ▼▼▼▼▼▼▼▼▼▼▼▼▼▼▼▼

Underline the verb or the verb phrase in the sentences below.
▪ Circle whether each verb is active (A) or passive (P).

1. The leaves of the maple tree were falling.              A    P

2. The leaves were raked by the boy and his father.        A    P

3. Did you carry the gifts for the goddess into the temple?  A    P

4. Were the gifts for the goddess given freely?            A    P

5. Has the signal been given for the race?                 A    P

6. Will the news of the winner be announced today?         A    P

## 26. WHAT IS MEANT BY MOOD?

The word **mood** is a variation of the word *mode*, meaning manner or way. The mood is the form of the verb which indicates the attitude (mode) of the speaker toward what he or she is saying. As a beginning student of Latin, all you have to know are the names of the moods so that you will understand what your Latin textbook means when it uses these words. You will learn to use the various moods as you learn the verbs and their tenses and usages.

**IN ENGLISH**
Verbs can be in one of three moods:

The **indicative mood** is used to express or indicate facts. This is the most common mood, and most verb forms that you use in everyday conversation belong to the indicative mood.

> Jason *brought* back the Golden Fleece.[1]
> Medea *is* Jason's helper.
> *Did* Jason also *bring* back Medea?

The **imperative mood** is used to express a command (see p. 90).

> Jason, *bring back* the Golden Fleece!
> Medea, *help* Jason!

The **subjunctive mood** is frequently used to express an action that is not really occurring (see pp. 71, 92). It is the language of wish, possibility, condition, and other vague situations.

> The kings insists that Jason *bring* back the Golden Fleece.
> If Medea *were* loyal, she would not betray her father.
> Medea wishes that Jason *were* her husband.

**IN LATIN**
These same three moods exist and have their own special forms. Although the indicative is a common mood, as in English, the subjunctive is also very important in Latin (see **What is the Subjunctive Mood?**, p. 92). Most of the sentences you meet in the beginning of your study, however, will be in the indicative or imperative mood.

---

[1]Jason went to the land of Colchis to bring back the Golden Fleece. Medea, daughter of the king of Colchis, aided him, and he brought her back as his bride after a long journey. Eventually he left her for another woman.

*My sister is coming.*
Soror **venit**.
present indicative

*Sister, come with me.*
Soror, **venī** mēcum.
imperative

*My sister may come with us.*
Soror mea nōbīscum **veniat**.
present subjunctive

## 27. WHAT IS THE IMPERATIVE MOOD?

The **imperative** is the mood of the verb used for commands. It is used to give an order.

**IN ENGLISH**
There are two types of commands depending on who is being told to do, or not to do, something.

"You" **command**—When an order is given to one person or more, the dictionary form of the verb is used.

> Medea, *come* with me!
> Sailors, *be ready* to sail!

In these sentences neither *Medea* nor *sailors* is the subject; the speaker is merely calling out their names, but rather the subject is "you" which is understood.

"Let" **command**—When an order is given to oneself as well as to others, the word "let" or the phrase "let's" (a contraction of *let us*) is used followed by the dictionary form of the verb.

> *Let's* go!
> *Let them* die!

**IN LATIN**
The same two forms of commands exist. However, only the second person *you* command is expressed by the imperative mood. The "Let" idea of the first and third persons is expressed by the subjunctive.

"You" **command**—The command to a second person or persons uses the special form of the verb called the imperative, separated into singular and plural. The imperative singular is the present stem, and the plural is usually the present stem + **-te**. Consult your Latin textbook for the complete imperative forms of active verbs, as well as the imperative for passive verbs and deponent verbs.

> Mēdea, **venī** mēcum! [addressing one person]
>       imperative singular
> *Medea, come with me.*

> Argonautae, **venīte** mēcum! [addressing more than one person]
>        imperative plural
> *Argonauts, come with me.*[1]

---

[1]The Argonauts are sailors on the ship, the Argo, who sailed with Jason in search of the Golden Fleece.

"Let" **command**—This form is expressed by the subjunctive mood (see **What is the Subjunctive?**, p. 92) for the first or third person.

Vīvat! *Let him live!*

▼▼▼▼▼▼▼▼▼▼▼▼▼▼REVIEW ▼▼▼▼▼▼▼▼▼▼▼▼▼▼▼▼

Change the declarative sentences below to the imperative mood.

1. Students, you should listen to the story about the Argonauts.

_____

2. Sailors, you ought to sail with Jason.

_____

3. Jason, you should beware of Medea.

_____

## 28. WHAT IS THE SUBJUNCTIVE MOOD?

The **subjunctive** is a mood used to express a wish, hope, uncertainty or other similar attitude toward a fact or an idea.

**IN ENGLISH**
The subjunctive is only used in very few constructions. The subjunctive verb form is difficult to recognize because it is spelled like other tenses of the verb.

- in contrary-to-fact statements (see pp. 113-5)

    If I *were* you, I would go on vacation.
    Implication: But I am not you.

    She talks as though she *were* my mother.
    Implication: But she is not my mother.

    I wish that she *were* my teacher.
    Implication: But she is not my teacher.

- in clauses following verbs of asking, demanding and recommending

    I recommend that he *take* the course.
    instead of "takes"

    I demanded that she *come* to see me.
    instead of "comes"

    I move that the officers *be elected* annually.
    instead of "are elected"

These are just a few examples to show that English has the subjunctive form, but it is not used as frequently as it is used in Latin.

**IN LATIN**
In general the personal endings of the present subjunctive are the same as the endings for the indicative verbs, but the vowels before the endings change to indicate the subjunctive mood. There are only four tenses, in the active and passive voice, for the subjunctive: present, imperfect, perfect, and past perfect (pluperfect). There is no future or future perfect tense. Consult the your textbook for the complete forms.

As in English, Latin uses the subjunctive mood for contrary to fact statements (see **What are Conditional Sentences?**, p. 113) and in many subordinate clauses following verbs of asking, etc. (see **What is Meant by Direct and Indirect Questions?**, p. 110). However, there are many other independent and dependent uses of the subjunctive in Latin, and we refer you to the explanations and examples in your Latin textbook.

▼▼▼▼▼▼▼▼▼▼▼▼▼▼▼▼REVIEW ▼▼▼▼▼▼▼▼▼▼▼▼▼▼▼▼

Change each statement below to a contrary-to-fact statement starting "I wish that... ."

1. He was my father.

   I wish that _____

2. She was my daughter.

   I wish that _____

3. The rains will come.

   I wish that _____

## 29. WHAT IS A CONJUNCTION?

A **conjunction** is a word which joins words or groups of words.

> Jason *and* Medea fled from her father.
> *Neither* Jason *nor* Medea remained in Colchis.
> The lovers travelled over the sea *and* through many countries.
> Medea loved Jason, *but* he left her.
> They were happy *until* Jason wanted a new wife.
> Medea killed her children *because* she hated Jason.

**IN ENGLISH**
There are two kinds of conjunctions: coordinating and subordinating.

**Coordinating conjunctions** join words, phrases, and clauses that are equal in form; they connect or *coordinate* ideas of equal rank. Typical coordinating conjunctions are *and, but, or, nor, yet,* and *for.*

> good *or* evil
> connecting words

> over the sea *and* through many countries
> connecting phrases

> The sea was rough, *but* the lovers were happy.
> connecting clauses

**Subordinating conjunctions** join a dependent clause to a main clause; they subordinate one clause to another. The main idea is expressed in the main clause, and the clause introduced by a subordinating conjunction is called a subordinate clause (see p. 99). Typical subordinating conjunctions are *although, because, if, unless, so that, while, that, whenever,* and *until.*

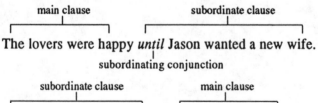

main clause    subordinate clause
The lovers were happy *until* Jason wanted a new wife.
subordinating conjunction

subordinate clause    main clause
*Although* the sea was rough, the lovers were happy.
subordinating conjunction

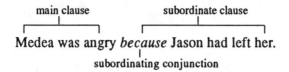

main clause      subordinate clause

Medea was angry *because* Jason had left her.

subordinating conjunction

Notice that the main clause is not always the first clause of the sentence.

**IN LATIN**

Conjunctions are to be memorized as vocabulary items. Like adverbs and prepositions, conjunctions are invariable; they never change. (They do not have case, number, gender, or tense.)

The major coordinating conjunctions are **et** *(and)*, **sed** *(but)*, **aut** *(or)*, **neque** *(nor)*, and **autem** *(however)*. Typical subordinating conjunctions are **quamquam** *(although)*, **quod** *(because)*, **quia** *(because)*, **sī** *(if)*, **cum** *(when)*, **ubi** *(when)*, **ut** *(so that)*, **dum** *(while)*, and **postquam** *(after)*.

Some subordinating conjunctions require the use of the indicative mood for the verb which follows, others the use of the subjunctive mood. Some are followed by either mood, depending on the meaning of the sentence. When you learn a new conjunction, be sure to memorize what mood it governs.

## Subordinating Conjunction or Preposition?

It is important that you learn to distinguish between a word functioning as a subordinating conjunction and as a preposition because occasionally the same word can be used in English, but two different words must be used in Latin.

For instance, *before* can be used as a subordinating conjunction and as a preposition in English. In Latin, however, as a subordinating conjunction *before* is **antequam**, but **ante** as a preposition.

We can distinguish between a preposition and a subordinating conjunction simply by determining if the word introduces a prepositional phrase (see pp. 98, 166) or a subordinate clause (see p. 99).

prepositional phrase

*Medea loved Jason **before** their departure.*

preposition     object of preposition

Mēdēa Iāsonem amāvit **ante** discessum.

preposition   object of preposition

subordinate clause

*Medea loved Jason **before** he loved another woman.*

|| subject verb object

subordinating
conjunction

Mēdēa Iāsonem amābat **antequam** aliam fēminam amāvit.

subordinating object verb
conjunction

prepositional phrase

***After** the voyage, Jason and Medea lived in Greece.*

preposition + object of preposition

**Post** nāvigātiōnem, Iāson et Mēdēa in Graeciā habitābant.

preposition + object of preposition

subordinate clause

***After** the voyage was over, Jason and Medea lived in Greece.*

subordinating subject verb
conjunction

**Postquam** nāvigātio fīnīta est, Iāson et Mēdēa in Graeciā habitābant.

subordinating subject verb
conjunction

▼▼▼▼▼▼▼▼▼▼▼▼▼▼REVIEW ▼▼▼▼▼▼▼▼▼▼▼▼▼▼▼▼

In the sentences below circle whether the boldfaced word is a preposition (P) or a subordinate conjunction (SC).

1. Theseus became king **after** he returned to Athens.          P     SC

2. **Because** he befriended Oedipus, his fame increased.          P     SC

3. **After** his father's death, Theseus ruled for many years.          P     SC

4. **Before** him stretched many years of service.          P     SC

5. **Because of** his wisdom, he became a famous king.          P     SC

6. **Before** he became king, Theseus had many adventures.          P     SC

## 30. WHAT ARE SENTENCES, PHRASES, AND CLAUSES?

### What Is a Sentence?

A **sentence** is the expression of a thought usually consisting at least of a subject (see **What is a Subject?**, p. 22) and a verb (see **What is a Verb?**, p. 45).

Atalanta lost.
subject  verb

The people were cheering.
subject   verb phrase

How did Hippomenes win?[1]
      subject
      verb phrase

Depending on the verb, a sentence may also have direct and indirect objects (see **What are Objects?**, p. 29).

Atalanta lost the race.
subject  verb  direct object

The king gave him the reward.
subject  verb  indirect  direct
              object    object

In addition, a sentence may include various kinds of modifiers: adjectives (see **What is an Adjective?**, p. 116), adverbs (see **What is an Adverb?**, p. 142), prepositional phrases (see **What is a Preposition?**, p. 166), participial phrases (see **What is a Participle?**, p. 73). Modifiers are adjectival if they modify nouns. Modifiers are adverbial if they modify verbs.

Atalanta lost the *long* race.
                 adjective

*Eventually* Atalanta lost the long race.
adverb

[1] All the young men who wanted to marry Atalanta had to race with her. Hippomenes distracted Atalanta by throwing three golden apples, one at a time, along the course, thereby winning the race and the bride.

Eventually Atalanta lost the long race *because of her curiosity*.

                                         adverbial prepositional phrase
                                         telling why Atalanta lost

Eventually Atalanta, *delayed by the apples*, lost the long race because

                         adjectival participial phrase
                         modifying Atalanta

of her curiosity.

Although not all of these elements of a sentence occur in Latin in the same way that they do in English, you will find it helpful to recognize the different parts of a sentence. Moreover, it is important for you to recognize complete sentences and to distinguish phrases and clauses from complete sentences.

## What Is a Phrase?

A **phrase** is a group of two or more words expressing a thought, but without a subject or a conjugated verb. It may contain an object. The various phrases are identified by the type of word beginning the phrase.

PREPOSITONAL PHRASE: a preposition + object of preposition

> *along* the way
> *after* the race
> *towards* the end

A prepositional phrase is adjectival if it modifies a noun, adverbial if it modifies a verb.

PARTICIPIAL PHRASE: starts with a participle

> *throwing* the apple
> present active participle of *to throw*

> *thrown* to the side
> perfect passive participle of *to throw*

A participial phrase is adjectival since it modifies a noun.

INFINITIVE PHRASE: starts with an infinitive

*to learn* Latin
infinitive    object of *to learn*

*to win* the race dishonestly
infinitive    adverb modifying *to win*

VERB PHRASE: starts with auxiliary verb or word (see p. 69 for details)

To recognize such phrases you need to recognize the individual parts (prepositions, participles, infinitives) and then isolate all those words within groups of words which work as a unit of meaning. If this unit of meaning does not have both a subject and a conjugated verb, it is a phrase.

## What Is a Clause?

A **clause** is a group of words containing a subject and a conjugated verb. It forms part of a compound or complex sentence (see p. 100).

There are two kinds of clauses: main (or independent) and subordinate (or dependent).

A **main clause** generally expresses a complete thought, the important idea of the sentence. If it stood alone with a capitalized first word and a period at the end, it could be a simple sentence.

A **subordinate clause** cannot stand alone as a complete sentence. It must always be combined with a main clause.

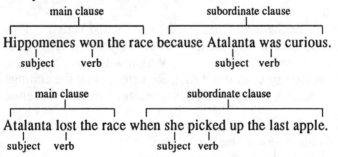

A subordinate clause is adjectival if it modifies a noun, adverbial if it modifies a verb.

## Types of Sentences

Let us look at the three types of sentences: simple, compound, and complex.

1. A **simple sentence** is one consisting of only one main clause with no subordinate clause. It has a subject and a conjugated verb. There may be many modifiers with a variety of word order.

**IN ENGLISH**

There is no set position for the verb in an English sentence or clause, but the subject usually comes before the verb, except in questions.

> Atalanta loved the winner.
>     subject   verb

Some other modifier can come before the subject.

> Secretly Atalanta loved the winner.
>   adverb

In questions, the word order varies from the normal simple sentence order.

> Did Atalanta love Hippomenes?
>      subject
> └─ verb phrase ─┘

**IN LATIN**

In a simple declarative sentence, the conjugated verb usually stands last. The subject usually stands near the beginning. This word order may vary, however, according to which words are being stressed and the verb may even stand first. Remember that the endings indicate the relationship of words and ideas in the sentence (see p. 14).

> Atalanta victōrem **amābat**.
>  subject   object   verb
> *Atalanta **loved** the winner.*

A variety of word order is possible depending on what is being stressed.

*Even before the race Atalanta loved the winner.*
**Etiam ante certāmen** Atalanta victōrem amābat.
The time element, "even before the race," is being stressed.

**Victōrem** Atalanta etiam ante certāmen amābat.
The *winner* is being stressed. Atalanta loved him and not someone else.

In a question, the ending **-ne** is usually attached to the first word, and since the verb is such a strong element in the sentence, it often stands first with the **-ne** ending.

**Amābatne** Atalanta victōrem etiam ante certāmen?
|
verb + **-ne**

*Did Atalanta love the winner even before the race?*

In spite of the modifiers, the above are all simple sentences.

2. A compound sentence consists of two statements or equal main clauses. These two statements are joined by coordinating conjunctions (see **What is a Conjunction?**, p. 94).

**IN ENGLISH**
The two main clauses are connected by a coordinating conjunction. Each clause has its own subject and conjugated verb. Each, standing alone, could be a simple sentence.

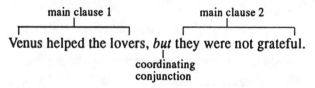

Venus helped the lovers, *but* they were not grateful.

**IN LATIN**
As in English, the two main clauses are connected by a coordinating conjunction.

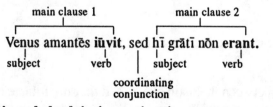

Venus amantēs iūvit, sed hī grātī nōn erant.

*Venus **helped** the lovers, but they **were** not grateful.*

3. A **complex sentence** is a sentence consisting of a main clause and one or more subordinate clauses.

The **main clause** in a complex sentence generally can stand alone as a complete sentence.[1]

The **subordinate clause** cannot stand alone as a complete sentence; it depends on the main clause for its full meaning, and it is subordinate to the main clause.

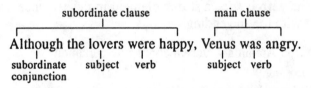

It makes sense to say "Venus was angry" without the first clause in the sentence; therefore, it is a main clause and could stand alone. It does not make sense to say "although the lovers were happy" unless we add a conclusion; therefore, it is a subordinate clause.

**IN ENGLISH**

It is important that you be able to distinguish a main clause from a subordinate clause. To do so will help you to write complete sentences and avoid sentence fragments. Subordinate clauses are introduced by subordinate conjunctions (see p. 94) or relative pronouns (see p. 159).

subordinate clause

Atalanta did not win *because* she picked up the apples.

subordinate conjunction

subordinate clause

Hippomenes threw apples *which* Venus had given him.

relative pronoun

All relative clauses are adjectival since they modify nouns.

**IN LATIN**

The distinction between the main clause and the subordinate clause

---

[1]Sometimes the main clause, though grammatically complete since it has a subject and a conjugated verb, cannot stand alone as a complete thought: *Hippomenes hoped that he would win.* "Hippomenes hoped" is incomplete without the subordinate clause telling what he hoped. Most main clauses, however, do express a complete thought.

is just as important as it is in English, and the same elements are involved.

In the main clause (which can stand first or last) the verb again is usually last in the sentence unless other words are being emphasized. A linking verb, however, does not necessarily stand last.

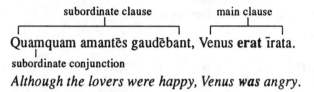

           subordinate clause              main clause

Quamquam amantēs gaudēbant, Venus **erat** īrata.
subordinate conjunction
*Although the lovers were happy, Venus was angry.*

As in English, subordinate clauses may be introduced by subordinate conjunctions or by relative pronouns.

            main clause            subordinate clause

Atalanta certāmine nōn superāvit **quod** pōma carpserat.
subject                   verb  subordinate conjunction
*Atalanta did not win in the race because she had picked up the apples.*

            main clause            subordinate clause

Hippomenēs dēiēcit tria pōma aurea **quae** Venus eī dederat.
subject     verb            relative pronoun
*Hippomenes threw the three golden apples which Venus had given him.*

The verb in the subordinate clause can be in the indicative or subjunctive mood (see **What is the Subjunctive Mood?**, p. 92).

Some clauses introduced by "that" following verbs of saying, knowing, thinking, feeling, and the like do not have verbs in either indicative or subjunctive; they have verbs in the infinitive. (See **What is Meant by Direct and Indirect Statements?**, p. 107.)

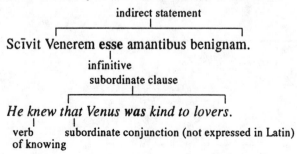

            indirect statement

Scīvit Venerem **esse** amantibus benignam.
         infinitive
        subordinate clause

*He knew that Venus was kind to lovers.*
 verb    subordinate conjunction (not expressed in Latin)
of knowing

▼▼▼▼▼▼▼▼▼▼▼▼▼▼REVIEW ▼▼▼▼▼▼▼▼▼▼▼▼▼▼▼▼

I. Circle whether the sentences below are simple (S), compound (C) or complex (CX).

1. The famous singer Orpheus loved ill-fated Eurydice.    S    C    CX

2. Orpheus married Eurydice, but his bride died
   immediately.                                           S    C    CX

3. Eurydice went to the Underworld, and Orpheus tried
   to bring her back.                                     S    C    CX

4. Because Orpheus looked back, Eurydice had to
   descend again into the Underworld.                     S    C    CX

II. Circle whether the following are phrases (P), clauses (C) or sentences (S).
   (All punctuation has been omitted.)

1. Orpheus denying all love of women and only
   singing his sad songs                                  P    C    S

2. Because the angry Maenads were throwing rocks
   at Orpheus                                             P    C    S

3. At first the rocks fell at the feet of Orpheus,
   conquered by the songs of the bard                     P    C    S

4. Finally the shouts of the Maenads and the drums
   overcame the song of Orpheus                           P    C    S

## 31. WHAT ARE DECLARATIVE AND INTERROGATIVE SENTENCES?

A sentence is classified according to its purpose, whether it makes a statement or asks a question.

A **declarative sentence** is a sentence that makes a statement.

> The Greeks invaded Troy.[1]

An **Interrogative sentence** is a sentence that asks a question.

> Why did the Greeks invade Troy?

In written language, an interrogative sentence always has a question mark at the end.

**IN ENGLISH**

A declarative sentence can be changed to an interrogative sentence in one of three ways:

1. Add the auxiliary verb *do, does, did, will* or *shall* before the subject and change the main verb to the dictionary form of the verb. *Do* and *does* are used to introduce a question in the present tense and *did* to introduce a question in the past tense (see **What is the Present Tense?**, p. 58 and **What is the Past Tense?**, p. 60) and *will* or *shall* to introduce a question in the future tense (see **What is the Future Tense?**, p. 65).

   **present**  Paris carries off the beautiful Helen.
   *Does* Paris carry off the beautiful Helen?

   **past**  The Greek leaders invaded Troy.
   *Did* the Greek leaders invade Troy?

   **future**  The Greek leaders will invade Troy.
   *Will* the Greek leaders invade Troy?

2. Some verbs allow you to switch the verb and the subject around, placing the verb before the subject. This reversing of the normal "subject + verb" order is called inverting or **inversion**.

   **statement**  *The Greeks are* now in Troy.
              S    V

   **question**  *Are the Greeks* now in Troy?
           V      S

---

[1]The Trojan War was fought to bring back the beautiful Helen from Troy, where she had been taken by Paris, a Trojan prince. The Greeks built the Trojan Horse as a device to enter the city and capture it.

3. A statement can also be transformed into a question by adding a short phrase at the end of the statement. This short phrase is sometimes called a **tag**. A tag is used when you expect a "yes" or "no" answer.

> The Greeks didn't invade Troy, *did they?*
> The Greeks are now in Troy, *aren't they?*

**IN LATIN**

Statements can be changed into questions by using one of the two following methods:

> **statement** Ducēs Graecī Trōiam invādēbant.
> *The Greek leaders were invading Troy.*

1. Adding **-ne** to the first word in the sentence. The answer can be either "yes" or "no."

> **question Invādēbantne** Trōiam ducēs Graecī?
> *Were the Greek leaders invading Troy?*

Often the verb appears first in a question, since it is the word being stressed in the sentence.

2. There is an equivalent to the tag used in English, but in Latin instead of being at the end it is placed at the beginning of the sentence: **Nōnne** is used when a "yes" answer is expected and **Num** is used when a "no" answer is expected.

> **Nōnne** Graecī Trōiam invāsērunt?        ["Yes" answer expected.]
> *The Greeks invaded Troy, **didn't they?***

> **Num** Graecī Rōmam invāsērunt?        ["No" answer expected.]
> *The Greeks did not invade Rome, **did they?***

▼▼▼▼▼▼▼▼▼▼▼▼▼▼REVIEW ▼▼▼▼▼▼▼▼▼▼▼▼▼▼▼▼

Change the following statements to questions.

1. Helen was the wife of King Menelaus.

_____?

2. The Trojan prince Paris carried off Helen.

_____?

3. King Menelaus was very angry at this outrage.

_____?

## 32. WHAT IS MEANT BY DIRECT AND INDIRECT STATEMENTS?

A **direct statement** is the transmission of a message by direct quotation. The message is set in quotation marks.

Caesar says, *"I came, I saw, I conquered."*
Cicero said, *"My city is in danger."*

An **indirect statement** is the reporting of the message without quoting the words directly. It does not use quotation marks.

Caesar says *(that) he came, he saw, he conquered.*
Cicero said *(that) his city was in danger.*

Notice in the first sentence above how the speaker's first person pronoun *("I came...")* in the direct statement changes to the third person pronoun *("he came")* to agree logically with the perspective of the person doing the reporting. Also, in the second sentence, the possessive adjective *"my"* has changed to *"his."*

### IN ENGLISH

An indirect statement is easy to recognize since the reported message is introduced by "that" forming a subordinate clause (see p. 103) used as an object of the verb of saying. No quotation marks are used. Frequently, especially in speech, the introductory word "that" is omitted.

Caesar says *(that) he came, he saw, he conquered.*
Cicero said *(that) his city was in danger.*

When the direct statement is transformed into a reported message, there is usually a shift in tense to maintain the logical time sequence in indirect statement.

| Direct statement $\longrightarrow$ | Indirect statement |
|---|---|
| | main clause    subordinate clause |
| Cicero *said,* "My city *is* in danger." <br>   past       present | Cicero *said* that his city *was* in danger. <br>   past       past |
| Cicero *said,* "My city *was* in danger." <br>   past       past | Cicero *said* that his city *had been* in danger. <br>   past       past perfect |
| Cicero *said,* "My city *will be* in danger." <br>   past       future | Cicero *said* that his city *would be* in danger. <br>   past    auxiliary "would" + verb |

**IN LATIN**

The construction of indirect statement is used not only after verbs of saying, but also after verbs of thinking, feeling, sensing, and the like. Latin uses no introductory word like the "that" of the English construction. Indirect statement is very commonly used in Latin and follows special rules distinct from those for direct statement.

As you can see in the indirect statements below, the subject of the indirect statement is in the accusative case and the verb is an infinitive.

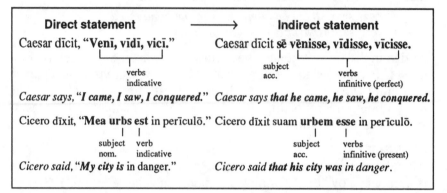

## Sequence of Tenses

Remember that there are three tenses of infinitives in Latin: present, perfect, and future (see **What is an Infinitive?**, p. 50). The tense of verbs follows a pattern called **sequence of tenses**. The infinitive tense selected for the indirect statement depends on when the action of the subordinate clause occurred relative to the action of the main verb.

PRESENT INFINITIVE: action of subordinate clause at same time as main verb

> *Cicero **thinks** (that) his city **is** in danger.*
> Cicerō **putat** urbem suam **esse** in perīculō.
>     present indicative        present infinitive

PERFECT INFINITIVE: action of subordinate clause before time of main verb

> *Cicero **thinks** that his city **was** in danger.*
> Cicerō **putat** urbem suam **fuisse** in perīculō.
>     present indicative            perfect infinitive

FUTURE INFINITIVE: action of subordinate clause after action of main verb

> *Cicero **thinks** that his city **will be** in danger.*
> Cicerō **putat** urbem suam **futūram esse** in perīculō.
>    present indicative      future infinitive

If we change the main verb from the present tense, "Cicero *thinks*," to the past tense "Cicero *thought*," the Latin infinitives would not change from what they are above, but they would have to be translated differently to maintain the time relationship between the main and subordinate clauses.

> *Cicero **thought** that his city **was** in danger.*
> Cicerō **putāvit** urbem suam **esse** in perīculō.
>    perfect indicative      perfect infinitive

> *Cicero **thought** that his city **had been** in danger.*
> Cicerō **putāvit** urbem suam **fuisse** in perīculō.
>    perfect indicative      perfect infinitive

> *Cicero **thought** that his city **would have been** in danger.*
> Cicerō **putāvit** urbem suam **futūram esse** in perīculō.
>    perfect indicative      future infinitive

Consult your text for a complete discussion of indirect statement.

▼▼▼▼▼▼▼▼▼▼▼▼▼▼▼REVIEW ▼▼▼▼▼▼▼▼▼▼▼▼▼▼▼▼

Change the direct statements below to indirect statements.

1. Cassandra says, "Troy is falling."

_____

2. Cassandra says, "Trojan women are slaves."

_____

3. Cassandra tells the king, "Your wife will kill us."

_____

## 33. WHAT IS MEANT BY DIRECT AND INDIRECT QUESTIONS?

A **direct question** is the transmission of a question by direct quotation using the exact words of the speaker. The question is set in quotation marks.

Paris asked, *"Where is Helen?"*
Helen wondered, *"When are the Greeks coming?"*
Priam asked, *"Who are the Greek leaders?"*
Paris wondered, *"How did I fail?"*

An **indirect question** is the reporting of a question without using the exact words of the speaker. It does not use quotation marks nor end in a question mark. It follows verbs of asking, knowing, doubting, wondering, and the like.

Paris asked *where Helen was.*
Helen wondered *when the Greek leaders were coming.*
Priam asked *who the Greek leaders were.*
Paris wondered *how he had failed.*

The word order is adjusted and any pronouns are logically changed to agree with the perspective of the person asking or wondering in the main clause.

**IN ENGLISH**

An indirect question is easy to recognize since the quoted question has become a subordinate clause introduced by the same interrogative word (*why, where, who, what, when,* etc.) that introduced the direct question.

There is often a shift in tense in the subordinate clause when the main verb is in the past tense.

| Direct question | ⟶ | Indirect question |
|---|---|---|
| Priam *asked*, "Who *are* the Greeks?" | | Priam *asked* who the Greeks *were*. |
| past        present | | past        past |
| Paris *asked*, "Where *was* Helen?" | | Paris *asked* where Helen *had been*. |
| past        past | | past        past perfect |
| Paris *wondered*, "How *did I fail* ?" | | Paris *wondered* how he *had failed*. |
| past        past | | past        past perfect |

**IN LATIN**

As in English, an indirect question is easy to recognize since the quoted question has become a subordinate clause introduced by the same interrogative word (**cūr**, *why;* **quis**, *who;* **quid**, *what;* **quandō**, *when;* **ubi**, *where;* **quōmodo**, *how;* etc.) that introduced the direct question. Indirect questions are very common in Latin and follow special rules distinct from those for direct questions.

The verb of the indirect question is in the subjunctive mood. The subjunctive tense selected for the indirect question depends on two factors:

1. the tense of the main verb (which remains in the indicative mood)

2. the time of the action of the verb of the subordinate clause relative to the action of the verb of the main clause

## Sequence of Tenses

The verb of the indirect question is in the subjunctive mood. Remember that there are only four subjunctive tenses in Latin: present, perfect, imperfect and pluperfect The tenses of the verbs follow a pattern known as **sequence of tenses** divided into **primary sequence** (when the main verb is in the present or future tense) and **secondary sequence** (when the main verb is in any past tense).

---

### SEQUENCE OF TENSES

| MAIN CLAUSE | SUBORDINATE CLAUSE |
|---|---|
| ↓ | ↓ |
| Indicative | Subjunctive |
| **Primary sequence** | |
| Present, future, future perfect | { present (same time or after main verb) or perfect (time prior to main verb) |
| **Secondary sequence** | |
| imperfect, perfect, pluperfect | { imperfect (same time or after main verb) or pluperfect (time prior to main verb) |

---

Let us see how this table works:

| DIRECT QUESTION ⟶ | INDIRECT QUESTION |
|---|---|
| **Primary sequence** | |
| Paris **rogat**,"Ubi est Helena?" | Paris **rogat** ubi Helena **sit**. |
| present     present | present     present |
| indicative  indicative | indicative  subjunctive |
| *Paris asks, "Where is Helen?"* | *Paris asks where Helen is.* |
| **Secondary sequence** | |
| Paris **rogāvit**, "Ubi est Helena?" | Paris **rogāvit** ubi Helena **esset**. |
| perfect     present | perfect     imperfect |
| indicative  indicative | indicative  subjunctive |
| *Paris asked, "Where is Helen?"* | *Paris asked where Helen was.* |
| Paris **rogāvit**, "Ubi **erat** Helena?" | Paris **rogāvit** ubi Helena **fuisset**. |
| perfect     imperfect | perfect     pluperfect |
| indicative  indicative | indicative  subjunctive |
| *Paris asked,"Where was Helen?"* | *Paris asked where Helen **had been**.* |

It is very important to learn the Sequence of Tenses table, since it is used in many subjunctive constructions, not only in indirect question.

▼▼▼▼▼▼▼▼▼▼▼▼▼▼▼▼REVIEW ▼▼▼▼▼▼▼▼▼▼▼▼▼▼▼▼▼

Change the direct questions below to indirect questions.

1. Clytemnestra wondered, " Why is my daughter being taken away?"

_____

2. Agamemnon asked, " Why is my daughter being sacrificed?"

_____

3. Iphigenia wondered, " Why are the priests standing there?"

_____

## 34. WHAT ARE CONDITIONAL SENTENCES?

The term "conditional sentences" refers to sentences which state that if a certain condition exists then a certain result can be expected. They are complex sentences (see p. 102) consisting of two parts:

1. a **condition**, the subordinate clause, which is introduced by *if* or *unless*

2. a **conclusion**, the main clause, which is the result of the condition

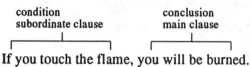

If you touch the flame, you will be burned.

**IN ENGLISH**

There are three types of conditional sentences.

1. SIMPLE CONDITIONS—The condition can take place in the present, past, or future.

   **present**    If you *say* this, you *are mistaken.*
   present         present

   **past**    If you *said* this, you *were mistaken.*
   past         past

   **future**    If you *say* this, you *will be mistaken.*
   present         future

   Although the present tense is used, a future time is implied.

2. "SHOULD-WOULD" CONDITIONS—Some doubt is implied about the possibility of the condition occurring, as expressed by the "should" in the condition and "would" in the conclusion.

   If you *should* say this, you *would* be mistaken.

3. CONTRARY-TO-FACT CONDITIONS—There is no possibility of the condition actually occurring; as the name implies, the condition is contrary-to-fact. These statements can only be made about the present or past.

**present**     If my friend *were* here, I would be happy.

                        subjunctive

                Implication: My friend is not here. *Were* is an example of one of the rare uses of the subjunctive in English (see **What is the Subjunctive Mood?**, p. 92).

**past**     If my friend *had been* here, I would have been happy.

                    past perfect indicative

                Implication: My friend was not here.

## IN LATIN

The same three types of conditional sentences exist with almost the same sequence of tense.

1. SIMPLE CONDITIONS—the indicative mood is used in both clauses in any tense.

Sī hoc **dīcis, errās.**

    present    present
    indicative  indicative

*If you say this, you **are mistaken.***

    present           present

Sī hoc **dīxistī, errāvistī.**

    present    perfect
    indicative  indicative

*If you said this, you **were mistaken.***

    past          past

Sī hoc **dīxeris, errābis.**

    future perfect  future
    indicative     indicative

*If you say this, you **will be mistaken.***

    present          future
    action 1        action 2

    Although the English present tense is used for action 1, a future time is implied (see p. 65). Since action 1 will take place before action 2 in the future, in Latin action 1 must be in the future perfect tense and action 2 must be in the future (see **What is the Future Perfect Tense?**, p. 67).

2. "SHOULD-WOULD" CONDITIONS—the subjunctive mood is used in both clauses. As in English, this condition implies some doubt about the condition occurring.

> Sī hoc **dīcăs, errēs.**
> present    present
> subjunctive   subjunctive

> *If you should say this, you would be mistaken.*

3. CONTRARY-TO-FACT CONDITIONS—the subjunctive mood is used in both clauses. As in English, here also, there is no possibility of the condition occurring.

> **present**    Sī amīcus meus nunc **adesset,** laetus **essem.**
>                            imperfect          imperfect
>                            subjunctive       subjunctive

> *If my friend were here now, I would be happy.*

> **past**      Sī amīcus meus herī **adfuisset,** laetus **fuissem.**
>                            pluperfect        pluperfect
>                            subjunctive      subjunctive

> *If my friend had been here yesterday, I would have been happy.*

▼▼▼▼▼▼▼▼▼▼▼▼▼▼REVIEW ▼▼▼▼▼▼▼▼▼▼▼▼▼▼▼▼

Circle whether the conditional sentences below are simple (S), should-would (SW), or contrary-to-fact (CF).

1. If the sailors go to the palace, Circe will
   turn them into pigs.            S    SW    CF

2. If Ulysses should go to the palace, Circe would
   be overjoyed.            S    SW    CF

3. If Circe were kind, she would not change
   men into pigs.            S    SW    CF

4. If Ulysses were home, he would not have to
   worry about Circe.            S    SW    CF

5. If Mercury should appear, he would save
   Ulysses and his men.            S    SW    CF

## 35. WHAT IS AN ADJECTIVE?

An **adjective** is a word that describes or modifies a noun or pronoun. Be sure that you do not confuse an adjective with a pronoun. A pronoun relaces a noun, while an adjective must always have a noun or pronoun to describe.

Listed below are the various types of adjectives and the sections where they are discussed.

**IN ENGLISH**
Adjectives are classified according to the way they describe a noun or pronoun.

A **descriptive adjective** indicates the quality of someone or something (see p. 118).

> Penelope lived in a *large* house.
> The stars are *bright*.

A **possessive adjective** shows who possesses someone or something (see p. 131).

> Aeneas loved *his* mother.
> Venus often gave comfort to *her* son.

An **interrogative adjective** asks a question about someone or something (see p. 136).

> *What* goddess did Niobe offend?
> *Which* child died last?

A **demonstrative adjective** points out someone or something (see p. 139).

> Cicero formed *this* plan.
> *That* senator praised the orator.

An **indefinite adjective** indicates the limits of someone or something, without being specific about those limits.

> *Some* Trojans escaped from the city.
> Did *any* hope of safety remain?

Since the use of the indefinite adjective in Latin closely corresponds to the English use, there is no special section devoted to this type of adjective. The Latin indefinite adjectives, however, have degrees of uncertainty which can easily be learned from your textbook.

**IN LATIN**

Adjectives also describe nouns and pronouns in various ways. The main difference from English is that in Latin the adjective always agrees with the noun or pronoun it modifies; that is, the ending of the adjective reflects the same case, gender, and number as the noun it describes. It may or may not have the same ending.

## 36. WHAT IS A DESCRIPTIVE ADJECTIVE?

A **descriptive adjective** is a word which characterizes a noun or pronoun.

**IN ENGLISH**
The descriptive adjective does not change form, regardless of the noun or pronoun it modifies.

> He has *bright* eyes.
> The *bright* star is beautiful.
> The farmer lives in a *large* house.
> We are looking at the *large* temple.

Descriptive adjectives are divided into two groups depending on how they accompany the noun they modify:

An **attributive adjective** usually precedes the noun it modifies.

> She lived in a *large* house.
> We are looking at the *bright* star.
> They have a *kind* teacher.

A **predicate adjective** follows a linking verb (see p. 25): *be, seem, appear, become*, etc.; it refers back to the subject.

> The house appears *large*.
> The stars are *bright*.
> The teacher seems *kind*.

**IN LATIN**
A descriptive adjective always agrees with the noun or pronoun it modifies; that is, the ending of the adjective reflects the case, gender, and number of the word described. It usually follows the noun it modifies.

> Oculōs **clārōs** habet.
>     └─┬─┘
>    acc. masc. pl.
> *He has **bright** eyes.*

> Stella **clāra** est pulchra.
>     └─┬─┘
>    nom. fem. sing.
> *The **bright** star is beautiful.*

Agricola in **magnā** casā habitat.

abl. fem. sing.

*The farmer lives in a large cottage.*

**Magnum** templum spectāmus.

acc. neut. sing.

*We are looking at the large temple.*

The gender, number, and case of an adjective depend on the noun it modifies. Although adjectives follow the same declension pattern as nouns (see **What is Meant by Case?**, p. 13), an adjective will only have the same endings as the noun it modifies if it belongs to the same declension. For example, an adjective of the first declension could be modifying a noun of the third declension leading to a difference in endings (see p. 121).

## Identifying an Adjective's Declension

There are two basic adjective declension patterns:

1. adjectives of the first and second declension which merge into a single group (called Group A in this handbook)

2. adjectives of the third declension (called Group B in this hand book)

When you learn a new adjective, see whether the dictionary entry has one, two, or three endings. If, for instance, it has the **-us** or **-er, -a, -um** endings, it belongs to Group A. All the others belong to Group B.

## Group A: Adjectives of the First and Second Declension

These adjectives are called "first and second declension" because the masculine and neuter forms are declined following the second declension and the feminine follows the first declension.

Most of the adjectives in this group are identifiable by their three-form dictionary entry ending in **-us, -a, -um**.

| | | |
|---|---|---|
| **dictionary entry** | bonus, -a, -um | *good* |
| **fully written** | bonus, bona, bonum | |
| | masc.  fem.  neut. | |

|       | Singular |      |       | Plural |      |       |
|-------|----------|------|-------|--------|------|-------|
|       | 2nd      | 1st  | 2nd   | 2nd    | 1st  | 2nd   |
|       | Masc.    | Fem. | Neut. | Masc.  | Fem. | Neut. |
| Nom.  | bonus    | bona | bonum | bonī   | bonae | bona  |
| Gen.  | bonī     | bonae | bonī | bonōrum | bonārum | bonōrum |
| Dat.  | bonō     | bonae | bonō | bonīs  | bonīs | bonīs |
| Acc.  | bonum    | bonam | bonum | bonōs | bonās | bona  |
| Abl.  | bonō     | bonā | bonō  | bonīs  | bonīs | bonīs |

There are several adjectives following this pattern whose nominative masculine singular ends in **-er**. Whether these adjectives keep or drop the **-e-** in the stem is apparent in the feminine and neuter forms given in the vocabulary entry. The rest of the declension is completely regular.

|                     | keep the **-e-**<br>↓ | drop the **-e-**<br>↓ |
|---------------------|------------------------|-------------------------|
| **dictionary entry** | **miser, -a, -um**    | **pulcher, -chra, -chrum** |
| **stem**            | miser-                 | pulchr-                 |

## Group B: Adjectives of the Third Declension

All the forms of these adjectives follow the third declension and are identifiable by the number of forms; i.e.,whether they have one form for all genders, two forms, or three forms. Consult your textbook for the complete declension.

Two FORMS—Most of the adjectives belonging to this group have two forms: the first for the masculine and feminine genders, and the second for the neuter.

| **dictionary entry** | fidēlis, -e | *faithful* |
|----------------------|-------------|------------|
| **fully written**    | fidēlis<br>\|<br>masc.<br>fem. | fidēle<br>\|<br>neut. |

ONE FORM—Some adjectives in this group have one form for all three genders. Since the stem of the adjective is not always seen in the nominative singular form, the dictionary entry also includes the complete genitive form.

| **dictionary entry** | audax<br>\|<br>masc.<br>fem.<br>neut. | audācis<br>\|<br>gen. | *bold* |

**Audāc-** is the stem of the adjective to which the endings are added.

THREE FORMS—Some other adjectives in this group have three forms, one for each gender. They can be distinguished from the three-form adjectives of Group A because they do not have that group's **-a, -um** endings for the feminine and neuter genders.

dictionary entry     ācer     ācris   ācre    *sharp*
                      masc.    fem.    neut.

**Ācr-** is the stem of the adjective to which the endings are added.

## Nota Bene

An adjective must agree with its noun in case, gender, and number, but its endings may be different from those of the noun it modifies, since the adjective may belong to another declension than the noun it modifies.

In **magnīs urbibus** habitāmus.
       adjective    noun
       2nd decl.    3rd decl.
       abl.fem.pl.   abl.fem.pl.

*We live in large cities.*

### Summary

Here is a chart you can use to determine the declension to which an adjective belongs on the basis of the number of forms listed in the nominative singular.

| Group | No. of Forms | Declension | Masculine | Feminine | Neuter |
|-------|------|------------|-----------|----------|--------|
| | | | | Nominative singular | |
| A | 3 | 1st | | bona | |
| | | | | misera | |
| | | 2nd | bonus | | bonum |
| | | | miser | | miserum |
| B | 3 | 3rd | ācer | ācris | ācre |
| | 2 | | fidēlis | fidēlis | fidēle |
| | 1 | | audax | audax | audax |

To make sure that your adjective has the proper ending, follow these steps:

1. NOUN MODIFIED—Analyze the noun's case, gender, and number.

2. DECLENSION OF ADJECTIVE—Determine declension of adjective.

3. CASE ENDING OF ADJECTIVE—According to the adjective's declension, choose the form of the adjective which corresponds to the case, gender, and number of the noun.

Here are a few examples to show you how to apply the three steps above:

> *Cicero was a **true** orator.*
>
> 1. Noun modified: *orator* → ōrātor
>    Case: nominative (predicate nominative)
>    Gender: masculine
>    Number: singular
> 2. Declension of adjective *true*
>    Dictionary entry: **vērus, -a, -um**
>    Gender of adjective: masculine since **ōrātōr** is masculine noun.
>    Declension: **vērus** → masculine Group A second declension
> 3. Case ending of **vērus**: **ōrātōr** is nominative singular →
>    **vērus** must be in the nominative singular.

Cicerō erat ōrātor **vērus**.

         nom. masc. sing.


> *Friends will aid the **unfortunate** neighbors.*
>
> 1. Noun modified: *neighbors* → vīcīnōs
>    Case: accusative
>    Gender: masculine
>    Number: plural
> 2. Declension of adjective *unfortunate*
>    Dictionary entry: **miser, -a, -um**
>    Gender of adjective: masculine since **vīcīnōs** is masculine noun.
>    Declension: **miser** → masculine Group A second declension
> 3. Case ending of **miser**: **vīcīnōs** is accusative plural →
>    **miser** must be in the accusative plural.

Amīcī vīcīnōs **miserōs** iuvābunt.

         acc. masc. pl.

*The **bold** Amazons terrified the men.*
1. Noun modified: *Amazons* → **Amāzonēs**
   Case: nominative
   Gender: feminine
   Number: plural
2. Declension of adjective *bold*
   Dictionary entry: **audax, audācis** (genitive)
   Gender of adjective: feminine since **Amāzonēs** is feminine noun.
   Declension: **audax** → feminine Group B third declension
3. Case ending of **audax**: **Amāzonēs** is nominative plural →
   **audax** must be in the nominative plural

Amāzonēs **audācēs** virōs terruērunt.

nom. fem. pl.


*Ulysses loved his **faithful** queen.*
1. Noun modified: *queen* → **rēgīnam**
   Case: accusative
   Gender: feminine
   Number: singular
2. Declension of adjective *faithful*
   Dictionary entry: **fidēlis, -e**
   Gender of adjective: feminine since **rēgīnam** is feminine noun.
   Declension: **fidēlis** → feminine Group B third declension
3. Case ending of **fidēlis**: **rēgīnam** is accusative singular →
   **fidēlis** must be in the accusative singular.

Ulixēs rēgīnam **fidēlem** amābat.

acc. fem. sing.


*Medusa was killed with a **sharp** sword.*
1. Noun modified: *sword* → **gladiō**
   Case: ablative
   Gender: masculine
   Number: singular
2. Declension of adjective *sharp*
   Dictionary entry: **ācer, ācris, ācre**
   Gender of adjective: masculine since **gladiō** is masculine noun.
   Declension: **ācer** → masculine Group B third declension
3. Case ending of **ācer**: **gladiō** is ablative singular →
   **ācer** must be in the ablative singular.

Medūsa gladiō **ācrī** necāta est.

abl. masc. sing.

As in English, there are attributive and predicate descriptive adjectives.

Attributive adjectives in Latin, in general, follow the nouns they modify, except for adjectives of size or quantity.

▼▼▼▼▼▼▼▼▼▼▼▼▼▼▼REVIEW ▼▼▼▼▼▼▼▼▼▼▼▼▼▼▼▼

In the sentences below, circle the following:
- the gender of the adjective in Latin: masculine (M), feminine (F), or neuter (N)
- the number of the adjective in Latin: singular (S) or plural (P)
- the case of the adjective in Latin: nominative (NOM), genitive (GEN), dative (DAT), accusative (ACC), ablative (ABL)

1. The heroic image of Hercules is a strong man.

*image*, **imago** → feminine; *man*, **vir** → masculine

| heroic | M | F | N | S | P | NOM | GEN | DAT | ACC | ABL |

| strong | M | F | N | S | P | NOM | GEN | DAT | ACC | ABL |

2. Mad Hercules killed his faithful wife.

*Hercules*, **Hercules** → masculine; *wife*, **uxor** → feminine

| mad | M | F | N | S | P | NOM | GEN | DAT | ACC | ABL |

| faithful | M | F | N | S | P | NOM | GEN | DAT | ACC | ABL |

3. Because he did an evil deed, Hercules had to perform harsh labors.

*deed*, **factum** → neuter; *labor*, **labor** → masculine

| evil | M | F | N | S | P | NOM | GEN | DAT | ACC | ABL |

| harsh | M | F | N | S | P | NOM | GEN | DAT | ACC | ABL |

## 37. WHAT IS MEANT BY COMPARISON OF ADJECTIVES?

When adjectives are used to compare the qualities of the nouns they modify, they change forms. This change is called **comparison**.

comparison of adjectives

The moon is *bright*, but the sun is *brighter*.

adjective modifying         adjective modifying
the noun *moon*              the noun *sun*

Both in English and in Latin there are three degrees of comparison: positive, comparative, and superlative.

**IN ENGLISH**

Let us go over what is meant by the different degrees of comparison and how each degree is formed.

1. The **positive form** refers to the quality of one person or thing. It is simply the adjective form.

> The philospher is *wise*.
> The moon is *bright*.
> The sword is *expensive*.
> His speech is *interesting*.

2. The **comparative form** compares the quality of one person  or thing with that of another person or thing. It is formed:

■ by adding *-er* to short adjectives

> The philosopher is *wiser* than many men.
> The sun is *brighter* than the moon.

■ by placing ***more*** in front of longer adjectives

> This sword is *more expensive*.
> This orator's speech is *more interesting*.

3. The **superlative form** is used to stress the highest degree of a quality. It is formed:

■ by adding *-est* to short adjectives

> This philosopher is the *wisest* in Athens.
> The sun is the *brightest* star in our heavens.

- by placing the *most, very*, or *exceedingly* in front of longer adjectives

    This sword is the *most expensive* in Rome.

    Cicero's speech is *very interesting*.

**IN LATIN**

Adjectives are compared in the same three degrees as in English: positive, comparative, and superlative. In all three degrees, adjectives are declined through the various cases according to their declension. Remember that, like all adjectives, they must agree with their noun in case, gender, and number (see **What is a Descriptive Adjective?**, p. 118).

1. The **positive degree** of the adjective is simply the vocabulary or dictionary form of the adjective.

    Gladius est ācer.

    noun — adjective
    positive degree
    nom. masc.sing.

    *The sword is sharp.*

2. The **comparative degree** is formed with the genitive masculine singular stem of the adjective in the positive degree + **-ior** (for the masculine and feminine) or **-ius** (for the neuter). These comparative adjectives are declined like the two-form adjectives in Group B (see p. 120) in the third declension. See your textbook for the complete declension.

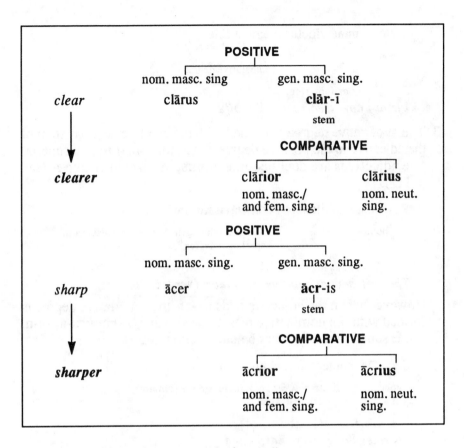

Hic discipulus respōnsum **clārius** dedit.

                noun         adjective
                           comparative degree
               — acc. neut. sing. —

*This student gave a* **clearer** *answer.*

Lingua est **ācrior** quam gladius.

     noun       adjective
                 comparative degree
    — nom. fem. sing. —

*The tongue is* **sharper** *than the sword.*

Adjectives whose ending is preceded by a vowel form their comparative degree with **magis** *(more)* placed before the adjective in the positive degree. For example, **dubius, dubia, dubium.**

Victōria nunc vidētur **magis dubia.**

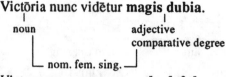

noun                adjective
                    comparative degree

         nom. fem. sing.

*Victory now seems **more doubtful**.*

3. The **superlative degree** is formed with the genitive singular stem of
the adjective in the positive degree + **-issimus, -a, -um.** All superlative adjectives are declined like **bonus, -a, -um** in Group A (see
p. 119).

Respōnsum philosophī erat **clārissimum.**

noun                        adjective (**clār-** gen. sing. stem + **-issimum**)
                            superlative degree

         nom. neut. sing.

*The philosopher's answer was **most (very) clear**.*

However, when the adjective ends in **-er,** the superlative degree is
formed with the nominative masculine singular + **-rimus, -a, -um.**
These superlative adjectives belong to Group A.

Sōcratēs mentem **ācerrimam** habēbat.

noun       adjective (**ācer** nom. masc. sing. + **-rimam**)
           superlative degree

     acc. fem. sing.

*Socrates had a **very sharp** mind.*

Adjectives whose ending is preceded by a vowel form the superlative degree with **maximē** *(most, very)* placed before the adjective in
the positive degree. These adjectives belong to Group A.

Victōria nunc vidētur **maximē dubia.**

noun                adjective
                    superlative degree

        nom. fem. sing.

*Victory now seems **most doubtful**.*

Consult your textbook for the few adjectives which form their superla-
tives in other ways.

## Summary

As reference here is a chart which summarizes the formation of the comparatives and superlative degree of the adjectives.

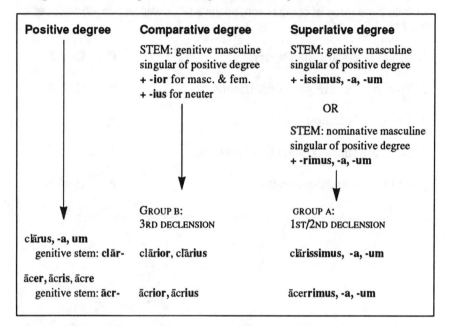

| Positive degree | Comparative degree | Superlative degree |
|---|---|---|
| | STEM: genitive masculine singular of positive degree + **-ior** for masc. & fem. + **-ius** for neuter | STEM: genitive masculine singular of positive degree + **-issimus, -a, -um** |
| | | OR |
| | | STEM: nominative masculine singular of positive degree + **-rimus, -a, -um** |
| | GROUP B: 3RD DECLENSION | GROUP A: 1ST/2ND DECLENSION |
| clārus, -a, um<br>    genitive stem: **clār-** | clārior, clārius | clārissimus, -a, -um |
| ācer, ācris, ācre<br>    genitive stem: **ācr-** | ācrior, ācrius | ācerrimus, -a, -um |

## *Nota Bene*

In English and in Latin there are several irregular comparisons of adjectives that are used frequently. These must be memorized, but since many words used in English are derived directly from the Latin, the task should not be difficult.

| Positive<br>(masculine) | Comparative<br>(masculine) | English<br>Derivative | Superlative<br>(masculine) | English<br>Derivative |
|---|---|---|---|---|
| bonus<br>*good* | melior<br>*better* | *ameliorate* | optimus<br>*best* | *optimist* |
| malus<br>*bad* | pēior<br>*worse* | *pejorative* | pessimus<br>*worst* | *pessimist* |
| magnus<br>*great* | maior<br>*greater* | *major* | maximus<br>*greatest* | *maximum* |
| parvus<br>*small* | minor<br>*smaller* | *minor* | minimus<br>*smallest* | *minimum* |

Consult your textbook for the other few, but important, adjectives that have an irregular comparison.

▼▼▼▼▼▼▼▼▼▼▼▼▼▼REVIEW ▼▼▼▼▼▼▼▼▼▼▼▼▼▼▼▼

In the sentences below draw an arrow from the adjective to the noun it modifies.

■ Circle the degree of comparison: positive (P), comparative (C) or superlative (S).

1. Blood is thicker than water.              P    C    S

2. Your parents are your best friends.       P    C    S

3. The poet is famous.                       P    C    S

4. Poets are more famous than soldiers.      P    C    S

5. Ovid is a most famous poet.               P    C    S

## 38. WHAT IS A POSSESSIVE ADJECTIVE?

A **possessive** adjective is a word which describes a noun by showing who possesses the person or thing being discussed. The owner is called the "possessor," and the noun modified is called the person or thing "possessed."

Whose house is that? It's *my* house.

"My" is the possessor; "house" is the object possessed.

**IN ENGLISH**

Here is a list of the possessive adjectives:

| Person | Singular | Plural |
|--------|----------|--------|
| 1st | my | our |
| 2nd | your | your |
| 3rd | his, her, its | their |

The possessive adjective refers only to the person who possesses, the possessor.

Aeneas was Venus's son. Ve̅nus loved *her* son.
   possessor

Aeneas's mother was a goddess. He loved *his* mother.
   possessor

Troy's walls were high. Tro̅y did not defend *its* walls.
   possessor

When the 3rd person singular *(his, her, its)* and plural *(their)* are used, two meanings are often possible. For example, the sentence "Medea murdered her children" could mean that Medea murdered her own children or someone else's. Usually the context of the sentence helps us understand the correct meaning; however, when there is a possibility of a misunderstanding, the word *own* is added after the possessive adjective: "Medea murdered *her own* children." In this case, and whenever *own* can be added after the possessive adjective, the possessive adjective is called **reflexive**; it "reflects back" to the possessor which is usually the subject of the sentence or clause.

The goddess saw *her* father.     [referring to her own father]

If the possessive adjective refers to a possessor other than the subject of the sentence or clause, it is called **non-reflexive**.

The goddess saw *her* father.     [referring to someone else's father]

**IN LATIN**

Like the English adjective, the possessive adjective refers to the possessor, but like most Latin adjectives, it must agree in case, number, and gender with the noun possessed.

Venus loved *her* son.
possessor   noun possessed

Aeneas loved *his* mother.
possessor   noun possessed

Troy could not defend *its* walls.
possessor            noun possessed

All the Latin possessive adjectives **meus, -a, -um** *(my)*, etc. belong to Group A (see p. 119). The third person possessive adjective **suus, -a, -um** is reflexive, and can only have the "own" meaning, *his own, her own, its own,* and *their own.*

Here are the steps you should follow to choose the correct possessive adjective and its proper form:

1. POSSESSOR: Indicate the possessor with the stem of the possessive adjective.

| | |
|---|---|
| my | **me-** |
| your (sing.) | **tu-** |
| his, her, its (own) | **su-** |
| our | **nostr-** |
| your (pl.) | **vestr-** |
| their (own) | **su-** |

2. NOUN POSSESSED: Identify the case, gender, and number of the noun possessed.

3. SELECTION: Provide the ending which reflects the case, gender, and number of the noun possessed.

*Citizens, the walls of your city are not high enough!*

   1. Possessor: 2rd person plural *(your* addresses many people, *citizens)*
   2. Noun possessed: **urbs** *(city)*
     Case: possessive → genitive
     *(Whose* walls are not high enough? Your *city's.)*
     Gender: feminine
     Number: singular
   3. Selection: **vestrae** genitive feminine singular

Cīvēs, moenia urbis **vestrae** nōn sunt satis alta.

*Aeneas loved **his** mother.*

1. Possessor: 3rd person reflexive
2. Noun possessed: **māter** *(mother)*
   Case: direct object → accusative
   (Aeneas loved *whom?* His mother.)
   Gender: feminine
   Number: singular
3. Selection: **suam** accusative feminine singular

Aenēas mātrem **suam** amābat.

*Venus often gave comfort to **her** son.*

1. Possessor: 3rd person reflexive
2. Noun possessed: **fīlius** *(son)*
   Case: indirect object → dative
   (Venus gave comfort *to whom?* To her son.)
   Gender: masculine
   Number: singular
3. Selection: **suō** dative masculine singular

Venus fīliō **suō** consōlātiōnem saepe dedit.

For the 3rd person non-reflexive adjectives, Latin uses the genitives of the personal pronoun **is, ea, id: eius, eōrum** and **eārum** (see p. 41) with endings reflecting the gender and number of the possessor. The literal meaning is *of him, of her, of it, of them,* i.e. **librī eōrum** → *the books **of them** (**their** books).*

*The goddess saw **her** father.*   [referring to the girl's father]
Dea patrem **eius** vīdit.
            |
            personal pronoun
            gen. fem. sing
            referring to *the girl*

Compare the meaning of the above sentence with one where the possessive adjective is used.

*The goddess saw **her** father.*   [referring to her own father]
Dea patrem **suum** vīdit.
            |
            reflexive possessive adjective
            acc. masc. sing.
            agrees with **patrem** *(father)*

## Nota Bene

Possessive adjectives are frequently omitted in Latin if there is no doubt as to who is the possessor. However, you should add them in the English translation.

Eurōpa cum amīcīs lūdit.
*Europa is playing with **her** friends.*

▼▼▼▼▼▼▼▼▼▼▼▼▼▼REVIEW ▼▼▼▼▼▼▼▼▼▼▼▼▼▼▼▼▼

Below are a series of English sentences with a Latin translation in which the ending of the possessive adjective has been left blank.

- Fill in the blanks by following the steps on p. 132.
- Complete the Latin possessive adjective.

1. We love our mothers.

POSSESSOR: _____

NOUN POSSESSED: _____

■ FUNCTION: _____ → CASE: _____

■ GENDER: _____

■ NUMBER: _____

SELECTION: _____

Mātrēs nostr ____ amāmus.

2. You love your mothers.

POSSESSOR: _____

NOUN POSSESSED: _____

■ FUNCTION: _____ → CASE: _____

■ GENDER: _____

■ NUMBER: _____

SELECTION: _____

Mātrēs vestr_____ amātis.

3. They love their (own) mothers.

POSSESSOR: _____

NOUN POSSESSED: _____

■ FUNCTION: _____ → CASE: _____

■ GENDER: _____

■ NUMBER: _____

REFLEXIVE OR NON-REFLEXIVE: _____

SELECTION: _____

Mātrēs su_____ amant.

## 4. The girls love their (boyfriends') mothers.

POSSESSOR: _____

NOUN POSSESSED: _____

■ FUNCTION: _____ → CASE: _____

■ GENDER: _____

■ NUMBER: _____

REFLEXIVE OR NON-REFLEXIVE: _____

SELECTION: _____

Mātrēs eōr_____ amant.

## 39. WHAT IS AN INTERROGATIVE ADJECTIVE?

An **interrogative adjective** is a word which asks a question about a noun.

**IN ENGLISH**
The words *what,* *which* and *whose* are called interrogative adjectives when they come before a noun and are used to ask a question about that noun.

*What* book is on the table?
|
noun

*Which* person is in the room?
|
noun

*Whose* book is on the table?[1]
|
noun

*What* and *which* are used interchangeably to ask for a variety of information about a noun:

- the name of a person or thing *(what is the name of...?)*

  *What* goddess did Niobe offend? The goddess Latona.
  *Which* city was conquered? The city of Troy.

- the kind of person or thing *(what sort of...?)*

  *What (sort of)* woman offended the goddess? A proud woman.

- the amount or degree of something *(how much...?, to what degree...?)*

  With *what* sorrow did the mother bewail her dead children?
  With the greatest sorrow.

**IN LATIN**
There are four types of interrogative adjectives and the one used depends on the type of information being asked about the noun. Remember that interrogative adjectives must follow the rules of agreement of all adjectives: they agree with the noun they modify in case, number, and gender.

---

[1]*Whose* can be either an adjective or a pronoun in English, but in Latin it is considered only a pronoun and will be discussed under interrogative pronouns, p. 145.

*What is the name of...?* → **qui, quae, quod** declined in all the cases like the relative pronoun. Consult your textbook for the complete declension.

*What goddess did Niobe offend? Latona.*
Quam deam Niobē offendit? Latonam.
```
 |      |
interr.  noun
adj. |
 |
acc. fem. sing.
```

*What kind of...?* → **qui, quae, quod** declined like the relative pronoun (see p. 159), or **quālis, quāle** declined as an adjective of Group B (see p. 120).

To ask for this type of information, Latin has two possible interrogative adjectives:

*What (kind of) woman offended the goddess? A proud woman.*
Quae mulier deam offendit? Mulier superba.
```
 |      |
interr.  noun
adj. |
 |
nom. fem. sing.
```

*With what (kind of) punishment did the goddess inflict her?*
*With a severe punishment.*
Quālī poenā dea eam affēcit? Poenā sevērā.
```
 |      |
interr.  noun
adj. |
 |
abl. fem. sing.
```

*How much, to what degree...?* → **quantus, quanta, quantum** declined as an adjective of Group A (see p. 119).

*With what (how much) sorrow did the mother bewail the dead children? With the greatest sorrow.*
Quantō dolōre māter puerōs mortuōs flēbat? Maximō dolōre.
```
 |      |
interr.  noun
adj. |
 |
abl. masc. sing.
```

*How many...?* → **quot,** which is not declined.

*How many arrows did Apollo shoot? Seven arrows.*
Quot sagittās Apollo coniēcit? Septem sagittās.
```
 |      |
interr.  noun
adj. |
 |
acc. fem. pl.
```

## Nota Bene

The word *what* is not always an interrogative adjective. In the sentence *"What is on the table?"* it is an interrogative pronoun. It is important that you distinguish one from the other, because in Latin different words are used and they follow different rules (see **What is an Interrogative Pronoun?, p. 145**).

▼▼▼▼▼▼▼▼▼▼▼▼▼▼▼REVIEW ▼▼▼▼▼▼▼▼▼▼▼▼▼▼▼▼

Circle the interrogative adjectives in the sentences below.
- Draw an arrow to the noun each adjective modifies.
- Circle the interrogative adjective that would be used in Latin:
   (A) **qui, quae, quod**, (B) **qualis, -e**, (C) **quantus, -a, -um**, (D) **quot**.

1. What man carried off Helen? Paris.          A     B     C     D

2. What kind of a man did such an  evil deed?
   An evil man.                               A     B     C     D

3. What kind of crime did he commit?
   An adulterous one.                         A     B     C     D

4. How much booty did Paris also steal?       A     B     C     D

5. How many years did the Greeks wage war?  A     B     C     D

6. How many Trojans did the Greeks kill?      A     B     C     D

## 40. WHAT IS A DEMONSTRATIVE ADJECTIVE?

A **demonstrative adjective** is a word used to point out a noun. It is called demonstrative because it points out a person or thing. The word *demonstrative* comes from the Latin **dēmonstrāre** meaning *to point out* or *show*, which also gives the English word *demonstrate*.

### IN ENGLISH

The demonstrative adjectives are *this* and *that* in the singular and *these* and *those* in the plural. They are a rare example of English adjectives agreeing with the noun they modify: *this* changes to *these* before a plural noun and *that* changes to *those*.

| Singular | Plural |
|---|---|
| *this* arrow | *these* arrows |
| *that* book | *those* books |

The distinction between *this* and *that* can be used to contrast one object with another, or to refer to things that are not the same distance away. We generally say *this* (or *these*) for the closer object, and *that* (or *those*) for the one farther away.

Cupid has two arrows. *This* arrow is sharp, causing love.[1]
showing contrast

*That* arrow is dull, causing love to flee.
showing constrast

"*These* arrows are my weapons. I do not use *those* weapons."
referring to                                                    referring to
arrows at hand                                              rocks at a distance

### IN LATIN

There are several types of demonstrative adjectives, and the one used depends on the relationship of the speaker to the object or person pointed out. They are all fully declined. Consult your textbook for the complete declensions.

---

[1]Cupid shot Apollo with his sharp arrow, causing the god to fall in love. The dull arrow shot into Daphne caused her to flee. Just as Apollo was about to overtake the maiden she was changed into a laurel, which Apollo made his sacred tree.

Once you have identified which types to use, remember that, being an adjective, the demonstrative adjective must agree with its noun in case, gender, and number. To choose the correct form, follow the steps on p. 122.

***This, these*** → to point out a noun near the writer or speaker in space, time, or thought → **hic, haec, hoc**

**Hoc** consilium est optimum.
dem.    noun
adj.
nom. neut. sing.

*This plan (**just given**) is the best.*

Lege **hōs** librōs!
dem.    noun
adj.
acc. masc. pl.

*Read **these** books (**which I have here**)!*

***That, those*** → to point out a noun away from the speaker or writer and the person spoken to → **ille, illa, illud**

Cicerō, **ille** senātor nihil dīcit!
dem.   noun
adj.
nom. masc. sing.

*Cicero, **that** senator (**over there**) is saying nothing!*

Glōriam **illārum** fēminārum memoriā semper tenēbimus.
dem.       noun
adj.
gen. fem. pl.

*We shall always remember (hold in memory) the fame of **those** women.*

***That, these*** → to point out a noun near or belonging to the person spoken to (frequently implying contempt) → **iste, ista, istud**

**Ista** fābula est mihi nōn grāta.
dem. noun
adj.
nom. fem. sing.

*That story (**of yours**) is not pleasing to me.*

**Iste** equus nōn valet.
   |     |
dem.  noun
adj.      |
    |
nom. masc. sing.

*That horse of yours is not worth anything.*

In addition to pointing out a person or thing, Latin demonstrative adjectives have other functions. Consult your textbook for other special uses of each demonstrative adjective.

▼▼▼▼▼▼▼▼▼▼▼▼▼▼▼REVIEW ▼▼▼▼▼▼▼▼▼▼▼▼▼▼▼▼

Circle the demonstrative adjectives in the sentences below.

- Draw an arrow to the noun each adjective modifies.
- Circle the demonstrative adjective that would be used in Latin:
  (A) **hic, haec, hoc**, (B) **ille, illa, illud**, (C) **iste, ista, istud**.

1. The Greeks planned to attack that city.           A    B    C

2. This plan was sure to work.                   A    B    C

3. These ships are ready to sail.                A    B    C

4. Those ships are still under construction.     A    B    C

5. I do not like those (badly built) ships (of yours).    A    B    C

# 41. WHAT IS AN ADVERB?

An **adverb** is a word that modifies (describes) a verb, an adjective or another adverb. Adverbs indicate manner, quantity, time, place, and intensity.

> Theseus fights *well*.
>        verb  adverb

> The labyrinth was *very* complicated.
>         adverb  adjective

> Ariadne fell in love *too easily*.
>        adverb adverb

**IN ENGLISH**

Adverbs can describe verbs, adjectives, or other adverbs in a variety of ways.

- adverbs of manner answer the question *how*. They are very common adverbs and can usually be recognized by their *-ly* ending.

    Theseus escaped *cleverly*.
    *Cleverly* describes the verb *escaped* - it tells you how Theseus escaped.

    Ariadne planned the escape *carefully*.
    *Carefully* describes the verb *planned* - it tells you how the escape was planned.

- adverbs of quantity, degree, or intensity answer the question of *how much* or *how well*.

    Theseus feared *greatly*.

- adverbs of time answer the question *when*.

    Theseus will come *soon*.

- adverbs of place answer the question *where*.

    The Minotaur looked *around*.

**IN LATIN**

Adverbs are invariable; that is, they never change form.

Some adverbs are formed from the adjective stems plus the ending **-iter, -ē** or **-e** to indicate that the word is an adverb.

Thēseus nāve **celerī** effūgit.    Thēseus **celeriter** cucurrit.
*Theseus escaped in a fast ship.*    *Theseus ran fast.*
                 |                                    |
            adjective                             adverb

Many adverbs, however, are very different from their adjective coun-
terparts, and you will have to learn them as vocabulary.

Just like adjectives, adverbs can have degrees: positive, comparative
and superlative. The meaning and the formation of these degrees of
adverbs are very similar to the meaning and the formation of the
degrees of adjectives (see **What is Meant by Comparison of Adjectives?**, p. 125).

The most common adverbs have irregular comparisons similar to
those of the adjectives which have irregular comparisons.

| **adjective** | bonus, -a, -um | melior, melius | optimus,-a,-um |
|---|---|---|---|
| | *good* | *better* | *best* |
| **adverb** | bene | melius | optime |
| | *well* | *better* | *very well* |

### *Nota Bene*

In English some adverbs are identical in form to the corresponding
adjectives:

Theseus ran *fast*.                    Theseus escaped in a *fast* ship.
         |                                              |
      adverb                                       adjective
modifes the verb *ran*                   modifies the noun *ship*

It is important that you differentiate between a word used as an adverb
or as an adjective so that you will know which Latin forms to use: the
invariable adverb or the adjective which agrees in case, gender, and
number with the noun it modifies.

▼▼▼▼▼▼▼▼▼▼▼▼▼▼▼▼REVIEW ▼▼▼▼▼▼▼▼▼▼▼▼▼▼▼▼▼

I. Circle the adverbs in the sentences below.
- Draw an arrow from each adverb to the word it modifies.
- Circle the part of speech of the word that the adverb modifies:
  verb (V), adjective (ADJ), adverb (ADV).

| | | | |
|---|---|---|---|
| 1. Theseus fought bravely. | V | ADJ | ADV |
| 2. Ariadne loved him well, but not wisely. | V | ADJ | ADV |
| | V | ADJ | ADV |
| 3. Theseus was too cruel to her. | V | ADJ | ADV |
| 4. He abandoned her very carelessly. | V | ADJ | ADV |
| | V | ADJ | ADV |

II. Circle whether the **boldfaced** word in the sentences below is an adjective (ADJ) or an adverb (ADV).

| | | |
|---|---|---|
| 1. This is a **hard** surface. | ADJ | ADV |
| 2. He worked very **hard.** | ADJ | ADV |
| 3. She sang **sweetly.** | ADJ | ADV |
| 4. I love **sweet** candy. | ADJ | ADV |
| 5. You have **hardly** touched your food. | ADJ | ADV |
| 6. This is an **easy** review. | ADJ | ADV |
| 7. Take is **easy.** | ADJ | ADV |

## 42. WHAT IS AN INTERROGATIVE PRONOUN?

An **interrogative pronoun** is a pronoun (a word used in place of a noun) which introduces a question; *interrogative* is from **inter** *(among, between)* + **rogāre** *(to ask)*.

**IN ENGLISH**
Different interrogative pronouns are used for asking about persons and for asking about things.

> *Who* is in the room?
> *What* is on the table?[1]

**Persons**
The interrogative pronoun to ask about persons has three different forms depending on its function in the sentence (see **What is a Personal Pronoun?**, pp. 37-42).

*Who* is the nominative form and is used for the subject of the sentence.

> *Who* wrote that book?
>   subject       direct object

> *Who* will help you?
>   subject       direct object

*Who* is considered singular followed by a singular verb, regardless if the expected answer is singular or plural.

> Who *is coming* tonight?
>     singular verb

> Mark *is coming* tonight.      [singular answer]
> Mark and Julia *are coming* tonight.    [plural answer]

*Whom* is the objective form and is used for the direct and indirect objects and for the object of a preposition (see **What are Objects?**, p. 29, 32).

> *Whom* do you know here?
>   direct  subject
>   object

---

[1]Do not confuse with *"What book* is on the table?"* where *what* is an interrogative adjective. See p. 136.

From *whom* did you get the book?
   |          |
object of   subject
preposition
*from*

In spoken English you will often hear *who* used instead of *whom* for the objective case. In order to establish the correct function it is important for you to distinguish between the function of *who* as a subject and *who* used incorrectly instead of *whom* as an object.

*Whom* is considered singular. The answer can be singular or plural.

*Whom* is the soldier killing?
He is killing *a warrior*.   [singular answer]
He is killing *many warriors*.   [plural answer]

***Whose*** is the possessive form and is used to ask about possession or ownership.

I found a stylus. *Whose* is it?
I have Mary's book. *Whose* do you have?

*Whose* can refer to one or more persons. The answer can be in the singular or plural.

*Whose* weapons are these?
They are the *soldier's*.   [singular answer]
They are the *soldiers'*.   [plural answer]

### Things
***What*** is used to ask about things. It does not change forms.

*What* is in the chest?
   |
subject

*What* are you doing?
   |
direct object

*What* is considered singular followed by a singular verb. The answer can be singular or plural.

What *is* in the chest?
      |
  singular verb

The treasure *is* in the chest.   [singular answer]
The treasures *are* in the chest.   [plural answer]

**IN LATIN**

As in English, different interrogative pronouns are used to ask about persons and to ask about things.

**Persons**

The personal interrogative pronoun is fully declined in all cases. Unlike English where interrogative pronouns are singular with a singular verb, regardless of the expected answer, Latin has a plural form for each case if a plural answer is expected. Some cases have a different form for the masculine plural and the feminine plural if the questioner expects an answer in one of the genders, i.e., a group of women (feminine plural), for instance.

To find the correct form of the interrogative pronoun, here is a series of steps to follow:

1. FUNCTION: Determine the function of the interrogative pronoun in the question to establish the case.

   - Is it the subject of the question?    *(Who?)* → Nominative
   - Does it show possession?    *(Whose?)* → Genitive
   - Is it the indirect object of the verb? *(To or for whom?)* → Dative
   - Is it the direct object of the verb? *(Whom?)* → Accusative
   - Is it the object of a preposition? *(With whom?)* → Ablative
                                            *(Against whom?)* →Accusative

2. NUMBER: Determine if the questioner is expecting a singular or plural answer.

   SINGULAR: If the context indicates that the questioner is expecting a singular answer, choose the form of the interrogative pronoun which corresponds to the case established under step 1 above. There is no gender distinction in the singular.

   PLURAL AND GENDER: If the context indicates that the questioner is expecting a plural answer, determine the gender of the expected answer. When the interrogative pronoun has a different masculine and feminine form, choose the masculine plural when referring to a group of all men or to a mixed group of men and women, or choose the feminine plural when referring to a group of women only.

Here are a few examples. Since the English question does not reveal if the expected answer is singular, masculine plural or feminine plural, context is provided between brackets for each question below.

*Who* → subject → nominative → **quis** (masc. and fem. sing.)
                                              **quī** (masc. pl.)
                                              **quae** (fem. pl.)

*Who is in the dining room?*
 1. Function of *who*: subject → nominative
 2. Number: singular

**Quis** est in trīclīniō? [Singular answer expected, i.e., one person in the room]
 |
 nom. sing.

*Who is coming today?*
 1. Function of *who*: subject → nominative
 2. Number and gender: plural masculine or feminine

**Quī** hodiē veniunt? [Plural answer expected, i.e., group of people]
 |
 nom. masc. pl.

**Quae** hodiē veniunt? [Plural answer expected, i.e., group of women]
 |
 nom. fem. pl.

*Whom* → direct object → accusative or dative → **quem** (sing.)
                                                 **quōs** (masc. pl.)
                                                 **quās** (fem. pl.)

The interrogative pronoun used as an object is more difficult to identify because *whom*, which is the standard form, has often been incorrectly replaced by *who* in colloquial language; make sure that you use the case required by the Latin verb.

*Whom do you see?*    [Singular or plural answer expected.]
 1. Function of *whom* : direct object
 2. Case: **Vidēre** *(to see)* requires an accusative object.
 3. Number: singular

**Quem** vidēs?
 |
 acc. sing.

*Whom is the soldier killing?*    [Referring to many men being killed.]
 1. Function of *whom*: direct object
 2. Case: **Necāre** *(to kill)* requires an accusative object.
 3. Number and gender: masculine plural

**Quōs** mīles necat?
 |
 acc. masc. pl.

*Whom are the children seeking?*    [Referring to their mothers.]
 1. Function of *whom:* direct object
 2. Case: **Quaerere** *(to seek)* requires an accusative object.
 3. Number and gender: feminine plural

**Quās** līberī quaerunt?
 |
 acc. fem. pl.

***Whom*** → indirect object → dative → **cuī** (sing.)

**quibus** (pl.)

Make sure that you restructure dangling prepositions (see p. 160).

***Whom shall I give the letter to?***    [Singular answer expected.]
Restructured: *To whom* shall I give the letter?

1. Function of *whom* : indirect object
2. Case: dative
3. Number: singular

**Cuī** litterās dābō?

dat. sing.

***Whom are you giving the gift to?***    [Plural answer expected.]
Restructured: *To whom* are you giving the gift ?

1. Function of *whom* : indirect object
2. Case: dative
3. Number: plural

**Quibus** dōnum dās?

dat. pl.

***Whom*** → object of a preposition → accusative or ablative. Choose the proper case based on the preposition.

| preposition (accusative) | + **quem** (sing.) |
| | + **quōs** (masc. pl.) |
| | + **quās** (fem. pl.) |
| preposition (ablative) | + **quō** (sing.) |
| | + **quibus** (pl.) |

***Whom are you fighting against?***
Restructured: *Against whom* are you fighting?

1. Function of *whom* : object of preposition
2. Case: contrā *(against)* requires the accusative case.
3. Number: singular

Contrā **quem** pugnās? [Singular answer expected.]

acc. sing.

Contrā **quōs** pugnās? [Plural answer expected; you are fighting against many men.]

acc. masc. pl.

Contrā **quās** pugnās? [Plural answer expected; you are fighting against many women.]

acc. fem. pl.

***Whose*** → possessive → genitive → **cuius** (masc. and fem. sing.)

**quōrum** (masc. pl.)

**quārum** (fem. pl.)

*I have his book. **Whose** do you have?*
 1. Function of *whose* : possessive → genitive
 2. Number: singular
**Librum eius habeō. Cuius habēs?** [Singular answer expected.]
 |
 gen. sing.

The Latin equivalent of the interrogative *whose?* is always an interrogative pronoun. Even if in English the question above were asked with the *whose* as an adjective: "*Whose* book do you have?" Latin would still use the interrogative pronoun, the word-for-word translation being "of whom": "The book of *whom* do you have?"

*I see jewels in the chest. **Whose** are they?* [The women's.]
 1. Function of *whose* : possessive → genitive
 2. Number and gender: feminine plural
**Gemmās in arcā videō. Quārum sunt?**
 |
 gen. fem. pl.

## Things
*What* → **quid** (sing.)
 **quae** (pl.)

The same system of cases applies to interrogative pronouns referring to things as to persons, but there is only one gender, neuter.

To find the correct form of the interrogative pronoun, follow these two steps:

1. FUNCTION: Determine the function of *what* in the question to establish the case.

2. NUMBER: If the context indicates that the questioner is expecting a singular answer, choose the singular form; if plural answer is expected, choose the plural form.

Here are a few examples:

*What is in the chest?*       [Singular answer expected.]
 |
subject
**Quid est in arca?**
 |
nominative singular

*What do you see in the city?* [Plural answer expected.]
 |
direct object
**Quae in urbe vides?**
 |
accusative plural

▼▼▼▼▼▼▼▼▼▼▼▼▼▼▼REVIEW ▼▼▼▼▼▼▼▼▼▼▼▼▼▼▼▼▼

Underline the interrogative adjectives and interrogative pronouns in the sentences below.

■ Circle whether each word underlined is an interrogative adjective (IA) or an interrogative pronoun (IP).

1. What do you want to see in Europe?          IA     IP

2. With whom will you travel to Rome?          IA     IP

3. What ship are you taking?                   IA     IP

4. To whom are you giving the letter?          IA     IP

5. Who is going with you?                      IA     IP

## 43. WHAT IS A POSSESSIVE PRONOUN?

A **possessive pronoun** is a word which replaces a noun and which also shows who possesses that noun.

> Whose house is that? *Mine*.

*Mine* is a pronoun which replaces the noun *house* and which shows who possesses that noun.

**IN ENGLISH**

Possessive pronouns refer only to the person who possesses, not to the object possessed.

> **example 1**    Is that your house? Yes, it is *mine*.
> **example 2**    Are those your books? Yes, they are *mine*.

The same possessive pronoun *mine* is used, although the object possessed is singular in Example 1 *(house)* and plural in Example 2 *(books)*.

Here is a list of the English possessive pronouns:

| | |
|---|---|
| mine | ours |
| yours | yours |
| his, hers, its | theirs |

**IN LATIN**

The possessive pronouns **meus, -a, -um,** etc. are declined in all cases. The forms are the same as those of the possessive adjective (see **What is a Possessive Adjective?**, p. 132), but since they are pronouns, instead of modifying nouns, they replace them.

To choose the correct form, follow the same steps as for the possessive adjective.

> Estne illa domus tua? Ita, est **mea.** [domus]
>                               └────┬────┘
>                             nom. fem. sing.
>
> *Is that your house? Yes, it is **mine.** [my house]*

> Suntne illī librī tuī? Ita, sunt **meī.** [librī]
>                                    └───┬───┘
>                                 nom. masc. pl.
>
> *Are those your books? Yes, they are **mine.** [my books]*

In each example above, the gender and number of the possessive pronoun in the second sentence are determined by the gender and number of the antecedent in the first sentence.

▼▼▼▼▼▼▼▼▼▼▼▼▼▼▼REVIEW ▼▼▼▼▼▼▼▼▼▼▼▼▼▼▼▼▼

Circle the possessive pronouns in the sentences below.

■ Draw an arrow to the antecedent of each possessive pronoun.

■ Put parentheses around the word in the first sentence to which the antecedent refers.

1. Are those your daughters? Yes, they are mine.

2. Is this your house? Yes, it is mine.

3. Is this not our country? Yes, it is ours.

4. Is this your dog? No, it is not mine, it is yours.

5. Are these your jewels? Yes, they are mine.

# 44. WHAT IS A REFLEXIVE PRONOUN?

A **reflexive pronoun** is a pronoun which is used either as the object of a verb or as the object of a preposition. It is called reflexive because it *reflects* back to the subject.

>   *Narcissus* looks at *himself* in the pond.

**IN ENGLISH**
Reflexive pronouns end with *-self* in the singular and *-selves* in the plural:

| Person | Singular | Plural |
|--------|----------|--------|
| 1st | myself | ourselves |
| 2nd | yourself | yourselves |
| 3rd | { himself herself itself | themselves |

Reflexive pronouns can have a variety of functions: direct and indirect objects, objects of a prepostion.

>   I cut *myself* with my sword.
>   *I* is the subject of *cut; myself* (same person) is the direct object.

>   You should give *yourself* a present.
>   *You* is the subject of *should give; yourself* (same person) is the indirect object.

>   They talk too much about *themselves*.
>   *They* is the subject of *talk; themselves* (same persons) is object of the preposition *about*.

**IN LATIN**

As in English, there are reflexive pronouns for each of the different personal pronouns (1st, 2nd, and 3rd persons).

| SUBJECT PRONOUNS | REFLEXIVE PRONOUNS | | | | |
|---|---|---|---|---|---|
| Nominative | Genitive | Dative | Accusative | Ablative | |
| | | | SINGULAR | | |
| 1 ego | meī | mihi | mē | mē | *myself* |
| 2 tū | tuī | tibi | tē | tē | *yourself* |
| 3 { is ea id | suī | sibi | sē | sē | { *himself herself itself* |
| | | | PLURAL | | |
| 1 nōs | nostrī | nōbīs | nōs | nōbīs | *ourselves* |
| 2 vōs | vestrī | vōbīs | vōs | vōbīs | *yourselves* |
| 3 { eī eae ea | suī | sibi | sē | sē | *themselves* |

Like English reflexive pronouns, Latin reflexive pronouns can have a variety of functions.

**Mē** gladiō meō secuī.
reflexive pronoun
direct object → accusative
*I cut **myself** with my sword.*

**Tibi** donum dare dēbēs.
reflexive pronoun
indirect object → dative
*You ought to give **yourself** a present.*

Contrā **sē** pugnāvit.
reflexive pronoun
object of preposition **contrā** → accusative
*He fought against **himself**.*

▼▼▼▼▼▼▼▼▼▼▼▼▼▼▼▼REVIEW ▼▼▼▼▼▼▼▼▼▼▼▼▼▼▼▼▼

Circle the reflexive pronouns in the sentences below.

▪ Circle whether each reflexive pronoun is the first, second, or third person singular (S) or plural (P).

| | | | | |
|---|---|---|---|---|
| 1. No one hates himself. | 1 | 2 | 3 | S | P |
| 2. All people love themselves. | 1 | 2 | 3 | S | P |
| 3. I see myself in the window. | 1 | 2 | 3 | S | P |
| 4. You see yourself in the window. | 1 | 2 | 3 | S | P |
| 5. We see ourselves in our parents. | 1 | 2 | 3 | S | P |
| 6. You see yourselves in your children. | 1 | 2 | 3 | S | P |

## 45. WHAT IS A DEMONSTRATIVE PRONOUN?

A **demonstrative pronoun** replaces a noun which has been mentioned before. It is called demonstrative because it points out a person or thing.

**IN ENGLISH**

The demonstrative pronouns are *this (one)* and *that (one)* in the singular and *these* and *those* in the plural.

This distinction between *this* and *that* can be used to contrast one object with another, or to refer to things that are not the same distance away. The speaker uses *this* or *these* for the closer objects and *that* or *those* for the ones farther away.

Cupid has two arrows. *This* (one) is sharp; *that* (one) is dull.

"*These* are my weapons," says Cupid. "I do not employ *those*."
| |
referring to the arrows                          referring to rocks
at hand                                          at a distance

**IN LATIN**

The demonstrative pronouns **hic, haec, hoc** *(this)* and **ille, illa, illud** *(that)* are declined in all cases, singular and plural. The forms are the same as those of the demonstrative adjective (see **What is a Demonstrative Adjective?**, p. 139), but since they are pronouns, instead of modifying nouns, they replace them.

The form of the demonstrative pronoun depends on a series of factors: the case is determined by the function of the pronoun in the sentence or clause; the gender is determined by the gender of the noun the pronoun replaces (the antecedent); the number is determined by the idea being expressed.

To find the correct form of the demonstrative pronoun, here are a series of steps to follow:

1. PRONOUN FUNCTION: Determine the function, and therefore the case, of the demonstrative pronoun.

   - Is it the subject?              →   nominative
   - Is it the direct object?        →   accusative
   - Is it an indirect object?       →   dative
   - Is it the object of a preposition? →   accusative or ablative
   - Is it the possessive modifier?  →   genitive

2. GENDER OF ANTECEDENT: Determine the gender of the antecedent.

- Is it masculine, feminine, or neuter?

3. NUMBER: Determine the number of the idea being expressed.

- If the idea is *this (one)* or *that (one)*, choose the singular form.
- If the idea is *these* or *those*, choose the plural form.

4. SELECTION: Select the proper form of the pronoun based on steps 1-3.

Here are two examples to illustrate these steps.

> *Cupid has two arrows.* ***This (one)*** *is sharp;* ***that (one)*** *is dull.*

> 1. Pronoun function: *This (one)* → subject → nominative; *that (one)* → subject → nominative
> 2. Antecedent gender: **Sagitta** *(arrow)* is feminine.
> 3. Number: *This (one)* and *that (one)* are both singular.
> 4. Selection: nominative feminine singular → **haec** and **illa**

Cupīdo duās sagittās habet. **Haec** est acūta; **illa** est obtūsa.

|      | | |
| --- | --- | --- |
| fem. | nom. fem. sing. | nom. fem. sing. |

> ***These*** *are my weapons," says Cupid. "I do not employ* ***those***."

> 1. Pronoun function: *These* → subject → nominative; *those* → object → accusative
> 2. Antecedent gender: **Arma** *(weapons)* is neuter.
> 3. Number: *These* and *those* are both plural.
> 4. Selection: nominative neuter plural → **haec** and **illa**

"**Haec** sunt mea arma," dīcit Cupīdo. "**Illa** nōn adhibeō."

| | | |
| --- | --- | --- |
| nom. neut. pl. | neut. | acc. neut. pl. |

▼▼▼▼▼▼▼▼▼▼▼▼▼▼REVIEW ▼▼▼▼▼▼▼▼▼▼▼▼▼▼▼▼

Circle the demonstrative pronouns in the sentences below.

- Draw an arrow to the word to which each demonstrative pronoun refers.
- Circle which gender and number you would use for each equivalent Latin pronoun: masculine (M), feminine (F), or neuter (N) and singular (S) or plural (P). (Where necessary the Latin word to which the pronoun refers along with its gender has been given.)

1. This is a stupid plan. (**consilium**, *n.*)     M    F    N        S    P

2. Those are not my daughters.     M    F    N        S    P

3. This is not a sharp arrow. (**sagitta**, *f.*)     M    F    N        S    P

4. That is not my boy friend.     M    F    N        S    P

5. These are our faithful wives.     M    F    N        S    P

## 46. WHAT IS A RELATIVE PRONOUN?

A **relative pronoun** is a word that serves two purposes:

1. As a pronoun it stands for a noun or another pronoun previously mentioned called its **antecedent.**

> This is the woman *who* caused the war.
>            |      |
>      antecedent relative pronoun

2. It introduces a **subordinate clause,** that is a group of words having a subject and verb separate from the subject and verb of the main clause (see pp. 99, 102). A main clause can stand alone as a complete sentence, a subordinate clause cannot.

>     main clause        subordinate clause
> This is the woman *who* caused the war.
>                 subject   verb

The above subordinate clause is also called a **relative clause** because it starts with a relative pronoun *(who)*. The relative clause gives us additional information about the antecedent *(woman)*.

**IN ENGLISH**
Different relative pronouns are used according to whether they refer to a person or to a thing.

**Persons**
The relative pronoun *who* is used when the antecedent is a person. It has different forms depending on its function in the relative clause.

*Who* is the nominative form used for the subject of the relative clause.

> This is the hero *who* won the war.
>           |
>      antecedent
>
> *Who* is the subject of *won.*

*Whom* is the objective form used for all objects in the relative clause. We have indicated it between parentheses because it is often omitted.

> This is the hero *(whom)* Hector killed.
>          |
>      antecedent
>
> *Whom* is the direct object of *killed.*

*Whose* is the possessive form.

Helen was the woman *whose* face launched a thousand ships.
      antecedent    possessive modifying *face*

### Things

The relative pronouns *which* or *that* are used when the antecedent is a thing. They do not change forms. We have indicated them between parentheses because they are often omitted.

This is the wooden horse *(which)* the Greeks built.
      antecedent    subject of relative clause

*Which* is the direct object of *built.*

Troy is the city *(that)* the Greeks destroyed.
      antecedent    subject of relative clause

*That* is the direct object of *destroyed.*

### Use of the Relative Pronoun and Restructuring Sentences

The relative pronoun enables you to combine two short simple sentences into one complex sentence (see **What are Sentences, Phrases, and Clauses?**, pp. 97-102).

### The relative pronoun as subject

**sentence A**    That is the hero.
**sentence B**    He won the war.

You can combine Sentence A and Sentence B by replacing the subject pronoun *he* with the relative pronoun *who.*

That is the hero *who won the war.*

*Who won the war* is the relative clause. It does not express a complete thought, and it is introduced by a relative pronoun.

*Who* stands for the noun *hero. Hero* is called the antecedent of *who.* Notice that the antecedent stands immediately before the relative pronoun which introduces the clause giving additional information about the antecedent.

*Who* serves as the subject of the verb *won* in the relative clause.

### The relative pronoun as object

**sentence A**  This is the hero.
**sentence B**  Hector slew him.

You can combine Sentence A and Sentence B by replacing the object pronoun *him* with the relative pronoun *whom*.

This is the hero *whom* Hector killed.

*Whom Hector killed* is the relative clause.

*Whom* stands for the noun *hero*. *Hero* is the antecedent. Notice again that the antecedent comes immediately before the relative pronoun.

*Whom* serves as the direct object of the relative clause. *(Hector* is the subject.)

In English, the object pronouns, whether referring to a person or a thing, are sometimes omitted.

This is the hero *(whom)* Hector killed.
This is the battle *(that)* Achilles won.

It is important that you reinstate them because they must be expressed in Latin.

### The relative pronoun as object of a preposition

**sentence A**  Helen is a beautiful woman.
**sentence B**  Paris ran away with her.

You can combine Sentence A and Sentence B by replacing the preposition + personal pronoun *(with her)* with the preposition + relative pronoun *(with whom)*.

Helen is the beautiful woman *with whom* Paris ran away.

*With whom Paris ran away* is the relative clause.

*Whom* stands for the noun *woman*. *Woman* is the antecedent. Notice again that the antecedent comes immediately before the relative pronoun.

*Whom* serves as the object of the preposition *with*.

In colloquial English, you could also combine the sentences A and B above by saying:

Helen is the beautiful woman Paris ran away *with*.

In order to reestablish the relative pronoun *whom*, which must be expressed in Latin, you will have to change the structure to avoid ending the sentence with the dangling preposition *with*. Placing the preposition *with* right after the antecedent *woman* will help you reinstate the missing relative pronoun *whom*.

Helen is the beautiful woman *with whom* Paris ran away.

Restructuring English sentences which contain a dangling preposition will help you to identify relative clauses and teach you the difference between the use of *who* and *whom* in English.

Venus is the goddess Paris    ⟶   Venus is the goddess *to whom*
gave the golden apple *to*.           Paris gave the golden apple.

Priam is the king we are      ⟶   Priam is the king *about whom*
reading *about*.                 we are reading.

### IN LATIN

The relative pronoun **quī, quae, quod** is fully declined, the case used depending on the function of the relative pronoun in the relative clause. The antecedent plays an important role in the selection of the relative pronoun. In Latin, it matters not only whether the antecedent is a person or thing, but also whether the antecedent is masculine, feminine, or neuter by grammatical gender (see pp. 7-8) and whether it is singular or plural. For example, if you have the word *island* as the antecedent of *which*, you must use the feminine singular relative pronoun since *island* is feminine in Latin.

*The island, which you see, is very beautiful.*
     |       |
antecedent  relative pronoun
     Gender of antecedent: **Insula** *(island)* is feminine.
     Number of antecedent: *Island* is singular.
**Insula, quam** spectās, est pulcherrima.
  |    |
antecedent  rel. pr. acc. obj. of **spectās**
     └ fem. sing. ┘

Consult your textbook for the complete declension of the relative pronoun, in all cases, singular and plural.

To find the correct relative pronoun follow these steps:

1. RELATIVE CLAUSE: Identify the relative clause.

- Add the relative pronoun if it has been omitted from the English sentence.

- Restructure the English relative clause if there is a dangling preposition.

2. ANTECEDENT: Find the antecedent in the main clause.

3. ANTECEDENT GENDER AND NUMBER: Determine the gender and number of the antecedent.

   ▪ Is it masculine, feminine, or neuter?
   ▪ Is it singular or plural?

4. RELATIVE PRONOUN FUNCTION: Determine the function and therefore the case of the relative pronoun within the relative clause.

   ▪ Is it the subject?                    ⟶  nominative
   ▪ Is it the direct object?              ⟶  accusative
   ▪ Is it an indirect object?             ⟶  dative
   ▪ Is it the object of a preposition? ⟶  accusative or ablative
   ▪ Is it a possessive modifier?       ⟶  genitive

5. SELECTION: Choose the proper form of the relative pronoun based on steps 1-4.

Let us apply the steps outlined above to the following sentences in order to select the correct relative pronoun:

*The woman **who** caused the war was Helen.*
  1. Relative clause: *who caused the war*
  2. Antecedent: *woman*
  3. Number and gender of antecedent: **Fēmina** is feminine singular.
  4. Function of *who* within relative clause: subject → nominative
  5. Selection: nominative feminine singular → **quae**
Fēmina **quae** causam bellī dedit erat Helena.

*Is this the kingdom **(that)** the Greeks destroyed?*
  1. Relative clause: *(that) the Greeks destroyed*
  2. Antecedent : *the kingdom*
  3. Number and gender of antecedent: **Regnum** is neuter singular.
  4. Function of *(that)* within relative clause: direct object → accusative
  5. Selection:  accusative neuter singular → **quod**
Hocne est regnum **quod** Graecī vastāvērunt?

*Circe, **whose** power was very great, kept Ulysses in her palace.*
  1. Relative clause: *whose power was very great*
  2. Antecedent: *Circe*
  3. Number and gender of antecedent: **Circe** is feminine singular.
  4. Function of *whose* within relative clause: possessive modifier connecting Circe with her power → genitive
  5. Selection: genitive feminine singular → **cuius**
Circē, **cuius** potentia erat maxima, Ulixem in rēgiā retinēbat.

*Where is the woman you ran away with?*
Restructured: Where is the woman **with whom** you ran away?
1. Relative clause: *with whom you ran away*
2. Antecedent: *woman*
3. Number and gender of antecedent: Fēmina is feminine singular.
4. Function of *whom* within relative clause: object of
   preposition *with.* Cum always takes an ablative object.
5. Selection: ablative feminine singular → quā

Ubi est fēmina **quācum** confūgistī?
(**cum quā**) **cum** is attached to its pronoun object

*The temples (which) we are visiting are very beautiful.*
1. Relative clause: *(which) we are visiting*
2. Antecedent: *temples*
3. Number and gender of antecedent: **Templa** is neuter plural.
4. Function of *which* within relative clause: direct object → accusative
5. Selection: accusative neuter plural → **quae**

Templa **quae** vīsitāmus sunt pulcherrima.

*These are the swords you were talking about.*
Restructured: These are the swords *about which* you were talking.
1. Relative clause: *about which you were talking*
2. Antecedent: *swords*
3. Number and gender of antecedent: **Gladiī** is masculine plural.
4. Function of *which* within relative clause: object of preposition
   **Dē** always takes the ablative case.
5. Selection: ablative masculine plural → **quibus**

Hī sunt gladiī dē **quibus** loquēbāris.

## Nota Bene

With regard to relative pronouns, it is important that you remember
the following: 1. Although the relative pronouns *who, whom, which*
and *that* are sometimes omitted in English, they must always be
expressed in Latin. 2. In Latin, the relative pronoun takes it gender and
number from its antecedent, but its case from its use in its own clause.

▼▼▼▼▼▼▼▼▼▼▼▼▼▼REVIEW ▼▼▼▼▼▼▼▼▼▼▼▼▼▼▼▼

I. Restructure the sentences below to avoid dangling prepositions.

1. This is the hero we were talking about.

_____

2. Aeneas is the leader they came with.

_____

3. Dido is the queen he gave gifts to.

_____

II. Fill in "who" or "whom" in the sentences below.

1. Aeneas married Dido _____ loved him.

2. Aeneas married Dido _____ he later abandoned.

3. Aeneas heeded the words of Mercury _____ he respected.

4. Mercury reminded Aeneas about the gods _____ he had neglected.

## 47. WHAT IS A PREPOSITION?

A **preposition** is a word which shows the relationship between a noun or pronoun and another word in the sentence. Prepositions may indicate position, direction, time, manner, means or agent.

**IN ENGLISH**

The noun or pronoun which the preposition connects to the rest of the sentence is called the **object of the preposition**. Together they make up a **prepositional phrase**. Here are examples of prepositional phrases.

- to show position

  Danae was imprisoned *in a dungeon.*

- to show direction

  Jupiter came *to her* in a shower of gold.

- to show time

  Perseus lived *for many years* on the island.

- to show manner

  Danae reacted *with disgust.*

- to show means

  Perseus killed Medusa *with a sword.*

- to show agent

  Perseus was given winged sandals *by the god Mercury.*

To help you recognize prepositional phrases, here is a story where the prepositional phrases are in *italics* and the preposition which introduces each phrase is in **boldface**.

Because it was foretold that his grandson would kill him, the king *of Argos* imprisoned his daughter Danae *in a dungeon* so that she would not bear a child. Jupiter, the king *of the gods,* fell *in love* **with** *her* and came *to her* *in her prison* *in a shower of gold.* She bore the hero Perseus, but both mother and child were set adrift *in a chest* *on water.* The chest drifted *to an island* where the two were rescued and taken *to the king.* That king fell *in love* **with** *Danae* and wanted to marry her. When Perseus, now grown, objected the king sent him to bring back the head *of Medusa.* Eventually Perseus did kill his grandfather *by accident.*

**IN LATIN**

When you learn a preposition, you must also learn which case it requires for its object, the accusative or the ablative.

Below are two examples of prepositions and their objects.

> Arca **ad īnsulam** portāta est.
> acc. fem. sing.
>
> **Ad** *(toward)* always requires an accusative object.
> *The chest was carried **toward an island**.*

> Arca **ā piscatōre** inventa est.
> abl. masc. sing.
>
> **A** or **ab** *(by)* always requires an ablative object.
> *The chest was found **by a fisherman**.*

Some prepositions can take both the accusative or the ablative depending on the way the preposition is used. The preposition **in** *(in, on)*, for instance, is followed by the accusative when motion is indicated by the verb or the ablative when there is no motion.

> *Danae remained **on the island**.*
> Danaē **in īnsulā** mānsit.
> abl. fem. sing.
>
> **In** governs the ablative since there is no motion in the verb.

> *The chest was thrown **into the water**.*
> Arca **in aquam** iacta est.
> acc. fem. sing.
>
> **In** governs the accusative since there is motion in the verb.

## *Nota Bene*

In learning how to use Latin prepositions, there are several important rules to remember.

1. You must be careful to distinguish in English between prepositional phrases introduced by *to* indicating the indirect object (see p. 30) and *to* indicating direction toward a location.

   - *to* indicating an indirect object → dative

     The action of the verb is done to or for someone or something. The prepositional phrase answers the question *to what?* or *to whom?* The indirect object can be expressed either by *to* or by reversing the word order and putting the indirect object without the *to* before the direct object (see pp. 30-1).

> *He gave a theater **to the city**.*
> *He gave **the city** a theater.*
>> He gave the theater *to what?* To the city.
>> *The city* is the indirect object.

**Urbī** theātrum dōnāvit.
|
indirect object → dat. fem. sing.

- *to* indicating direction toward a location → **ad** + accusative case

  The preposition *to* is used in a phrase of direction towards a location. It answers the question *to where?*

  > *He was walking **to the city**.*
  >> He was walking *to where?* To the city.
  >> *The city* is the object of the preposition *to*.
  >> **Ad** *(to)* is followed by the location or destination in the accusative case.

  **Ad urbem** ambulābat.
  |
  object of preposition **ad** → acc. fem. sing.

2. Every language uses prepositions differently. Do not assume that the same preposition is used in Latin as in English, or that one is even used at all (see p. 33).

3. The Latin case system makes many prepositions which must be used in English unnecessary in Latin (see **What is Meant by Case?**, pp. 13-6).

   - *of* (possessive) → genitive (no preposition)
     > *The mother **of the boy** is here.*
     > Mater **puerī** adest.

   - *with* (by means of) → ablative (no preposition)
     > *Perseus killed Medusa **with a sword**.*
     > Perseus **gladiō** Medūsam necāvit.

   - *on, at* (location) → locative (no preposition)
     > *They lived **at home**.*
     > **Domī** habitābant.

4. When expressing an English sentence in Latin, remember to restructure any dangling prepositions so that you can find the object of the preposition and put it in its proper case (see pp. 161-2).

▼▼▼▼▼▼▼▼▼▼▼▼▼▼REVIEW ▼▼▼▼▼▼▼▼▼▼▼▼▼▼▼▼

Underline the prepositional phrases in the sentences below.

▪ Indicate what each prepositional phrase would be in Latin: a prepositional phrase (PP), a dative case indirect object (IO), or a genitive case showing possession (G).

1. Mercury gave winged sandals to Perseus.          PP   IO   G

2. Perseus flew to Gorgon country.          PP   IO   G

3. Perseus cut off the head of Medusa.          PP   IO   G

4. Perseus returned with the Gorgon head.          PP   IO   G

5. Perseus gave the head to the king.          PP   IO   G

6. Perseus freed Danae from the power of the evil king.   PP   IO   G

# 48. WHAT IS AN INTERJECTION?

An **interjection** is a cry, an expression of strong feeling or emotion. It is *thrown into* (from the Latin **interjectum**) the sentence, usually at the beginning, and stands apart from the grammar of the sentence.

**IN ENGLISH**
There is a great variety of such emotional words, including most words of swearing and profanity. They belong to both written and spoken language, but are separated from the main clause by a comma; the sentence usually ends with an exclamation mark.

> *Ah,* how beautiful she is!
> *Alas,* wretched me!

**IN LATIN**
A similar variety of emotional words exists in Latin and includes the equivalents of expressions of awe, anger, and the evoking of a deity. An interjection is invariable; i.e. it never changes form.

> **A,** quam pulchra est!
> *Ah, how beautiful she is!*
>
> **Heu,** mē miserum!
> *Alas, wretched me!*

# Answer Key

**1. What is a Noun?** 1. Diana, goddess, moon  2. Phoebus Apollo, brother, god, sun  3. Mars, god, war  4. Juno, goddess, marriage, childbirth  5. deities, Mt. Olympus, Olympians

**2. What is Meant by Gender?** 1. F;  2. M;  3. N;  4. M;  5. F;  6. F;  7. M;  8. N;  9. F;  10. M

**3. What is Meant by Number?** 1. alumnae  2. alumnī  3. annī  4. templa  5. litterae  6. curricula  7. portae  8. animī  9. rosae  10. indicēs

**4. What are Definite and Indefinite Articles?** 1. The boy lives in the woods.  2. He does not have a house.  3. Wild animals take care of him.

**5. What is Meant by Case?** 1. N, Acc, Acc  2. Abl, N, Acc  3. N, G, N, Acc, D, G

**6. What is a Subject?** 1. Q: Who is the goddess of the sacred fire? A: Vesta → S   2. Q: Who tends the sacred fire?   A: Vestal Virgins → P   3. Q: What stands in the Forum?  A: temple → S

**7. What is a Predicate Word?** (*Linking verb*, predicate word, subject) 1. *are*, angry, goddesses  2. *is*, god, Apollo  3. *is*, daughter, Daphne  4. *is*, he, it  5. *are*, enemies, these

**8. What is the Possessive?** 1. Arachne's → PG  2. of Minerva → PG  3. of weaving → OG  4. of the gods → PG

**9. What are Objects?** 1. Q: The king abandoned whom?  A: His daughter → DO  Q: The king abandoned his daughter in what?  A: In the woods → OP  2. Q: Wild animals raised whom?  A: Atalanta → DO  3. Q: Atalanta went to what?   A: The palace → OP  4. The king gave what?  A: His blessing → DO  Q: The king gave his blessing to whom?  A: To Atalanta → IO

**11. What is a Personal Pronoun?** I. 1. vōs  2. eī  3. nōs  4. eās  5. eam  II. 1. feminine, singular, accusative  2. masculine, plural, nominative  3. neuter, singular, accusative

**12. What is a Verb?** 1. praises → v.t.  2. is watching → v.t.  3. was running → v.i.  4. loved → v.t.  5. will kill → v.t.

**13. What are the Principal Parts of a Verb?** I. 1. thought, thought  2. ran, run  3. drove, driven  II. **laudō**, I praise, am praising, do praise; **laudāre**, to praise; **laudāvī**, I praised, have praised, did praise; **laudātum**, having been praised

**14. What is an Infinitive?** ACTIVE: 1. to have eaten  2. to have written

3. to have sung PASSIVE: 1. to be eaten, to have been eaten 2. to be written, to have been written 3. to be sung, to have been sung

**15. What is a Verb Conjugation?** I. 1. āre → first 2. ere → third 3. ēre → second 4. īre → fourth 5. ere → third II. STEM: laudā-. Present tense: laudō, laudās, laudat, laudāmus, laudātis, laudant

**16. What is Meant by Tense?** PRESENT: I think PRESENT PERFECT: I have thought PAST: I thought PAST PERFECT: I had thought FUTURE: I shall (will) think FUTURE PERFECT: I shall (will) have thought

**17. What is the Present Tense?** 1. PROGRESSIVE: The girls are carrying the sacred water. EMPHATIC: The girls do carry the sacred water. 2. PROGRESSIVE: The Vestal Virgin is taking care of the sacred fire. EMPHATIC: The Vestal Virgin does take care of the sacred fire.

**18. What is the Past Tense?** IMPERFECT: was sitting, was sleeping, was, was, was working, was sleeping PERFECT: heard, sat up, barked, ran, called, arrived, found

**19. What is the Past Perfect Tense?** 1. -1, -2 2. -1, -2 3. -1, -2

**20. What is the Future Tense?** 1. ENGLISH: P, F; LATIN: F, F; 2. ENGLISH: P, F; LATIN: F, F; 3. ENGLISH: P, F; LATIN: F, F

**21. What is the Future Perfect Tense?** 1. ENGLISH: F, P; LATIN: F, F; 2. ENGLISH: FP, P; LATIN: FP, F; 3. ENGLISH: P, FP; LATIN: F, FP

**22. What is an Auxiliary Verb?** was asking, sent, asked, demanded, (*to drive* is an infinitive), was feeling, had requested, insisted, yoked, could feel, plunged, hurled, died.

**23. What is a Participle?** 1. growing, A; 2. left, VP; 3. desiring, A; 4. chosen, VP; 5. chosen, A

**24. What is a Verbal Noun(a Gerund)?** 1. hoping, P; 2. training, G; 3. training, VP; 4. escaping, G; 5. dancing, G

**25. What is Meant by Active and Passive Voice?** 1. were falling, A; 2. were raked, P; 3. did carry, A; 4. were given, P; 5. has been given, P; 6. will be announced, P

**27. What is the Imperative Mood?** 1. Students, listen to the story about the Argonauts. 2. Sailors, sail with Jason. 3. Jason, beware of Medea.

**28. What is the Subjunctive Mood?** 1. I wish that he *were* my father. 2. I wish that she *were* my daughter. 3. I wish that the rains *would come.*

**29. What is a Conjunction?** 1. SC; 2. SC; 3. P; 4. P; 5. P; 6. SC

**30. What are Sentences, Phrases, and Clauses?** I. 1. S;   2. C;   3. C;   4. CX. II. 1. P;   2. C;   3. S;   4. S

**31. What are Declarative and Interrogative Sentences?** 1. Was Helen the wife of Menelaus? 2. Did the Trojan prince Paris carry off Helen? 3. Was King Menelaus angry at this outrage?

**32. What is Meant by Direct and Indirect Statements?** 1. Cassandra says that Troy is falling.  2. Cassandra says that the Trojan women are slaves.  3. Cassandra tells the king that his wife will kill them.

**33. What is Meant by Direct and Indirect Questions?** 1. Clytemnestra wondered why her daughter was being taken away.  2. Agamemnon asked why his daughter was being sacrificed.  3. Iphigenia wondered why the priests were standing there.

**34. What are Conditional Sentences?** 1. S;   2. SW;   3. CF;   4. CF;   5. SW

**36. What is a Descriptive Adjective?** 1. heroic → F, S, Nom; strong → M, S, Nom;   2. mad → M, S, Nom; faithful → F, S, Acc;   3. evil → N, S, Acc; harsh → M, P, Acc

**37. What is Meant by Comparison of Adjectives?** 1. thicker → blood, C  2. best → friends, S   3. famous → poet, P   4. more famous → poets, C  5. very famous → poet, S

**38. What is a Possessive Adjective?** 1. our, mothers, direct object → accusative, feminine, plural, **nostrās** 2. your, mothers, direct object → accusative, feminine, plural, **vestrās** 3. their (own), mothers, direct object → accusative, feminine, plural, reflexive, **suās** 4. their, mothers, possessive pronoun → genitive (of them), masculine, plural, non-reflexive, **eōrum**

**39. What is the Interrogative Adjective?** 1. what → man, A;   2. what kind of → man, B;   3. what kind of → crime, B;   4. how much → booty, C;  5. how many → years, C or D;   6. how many → Trojans, C or D

**40. What is a Demonstrative Adjective?** 1. that → city, B;   2. this → plan, A;   3. these → ships, A;   4. those → ships, B;   5. those → ships, C

**41. What is an Adverb?** I. 1. bravely → fought, V;   2. well → loved, V; wisely → loved, V;   3. too → cruel, ADJ;   4. very → carelessly, ADV; carelessly → abandoned, V II. 1. ADJ;   2. ADV;   3. ADV;   4. ADJ  5. ADV;   6. ADJ;   7. ADV

**42. What is an Interrogative Pronoun?** 1. what → IP;   2. whom → IP;  3. what → IA;   4. whom → IP;   5. who → IP

**43. What is a Possessive Pronoun?** 1. mine → they (daughters); 2. mine → it (house); 3. ours → it (country); 4 . mine → it (dog); yours → it (dog); 5. mine → they (jewels)

**44. What is a Reflexive Pronoun?** 1. himself, 3, S; 2. themselves, 3, P; 3. myself, 1, S; 4. yourself, 2, S; 5. ourselves, 1, P; 6. your-selves, 2, P

**45. What is a Demonstrative Pronoun?** 1. this → plan, N, S; 2. those → daughters, F, P; 3. this → arrow, F, S; 4. that → boy friend, M, S; 5. these → wives, F, P

**46. What is a Relative Pronoun?** I. 1. This is the hero about whom we were talking. 2. Aeneas is the leader with whom they came. 3. Dido is the queen to whom he gave the gifts. II. 1. who 2. whom 3. whom 4. whom

**47. What is a Preposition?** 1. to Perseus → IO 2. to Gorgon country → PP 3. of Medusa → G 4. with the Gorgon head → PP 5. to the king → IO 6. from the power → PP; of the evil king → G

# INDEX